THE
ULTIMATE GUIDE
TO BECOMING A
SUCCESSFUL ESCORT

PAUL STAG

Grosvenor House
Publishing Limited

This book is published by
Grosvenor House Publishing Ltd
Link House
140 The Broadway, Tolworth, Surrey, KT6 7HT.
www.grosvenorhousepublishing.co.uk

A CIP record for this book
is available from the British Library

ISBN 978-1-80381-572-5
eBook ISBN: 978-1-80381-670-8

INTRODUCTION

Escorting or prostitution is always referred to as the oldest industry in the World and there is little doubt about that statement being true. Yet there is scant informative information on the subject and most definitely a shortage of worthwhile instructive knowledge from inside that industry to help others....but that changes now with this book.

Many guys and gals dabble with escorting at some point in their lives for a bit of extra cash, as a way to get through college or a bad patch or even to make a mundane existence a lot more interesting. Most people do not have a lot of success and end up with very few clients, the phone rarely going or having a miserable depressing time doing it feeling subhuman, sad and a number of other negative tropes. Sometimes the demons of chems take over or sex indeed any kind of intimacy becomes formulaic, unexciting, business-like or problematic with relationships etc. Yet if done properly it is a fantastic job...and it is a full-time career for many; where they meet loads of great people, have the most fantastic experiences, have sex with many celebrities, enjoy great company and make a veritable fortune along the way. Escorting can easily buy you a house, a great car, fantastic holidays and so much more and it can also last a lifetime with escorts trading successfully from 18 years old deep into retirement age. Therefore, if done right it is the dream job or part time job whatever works for you and this book will provide you with all the information you will need to become a top International escort, making loads of cash and being happy, horny, healthy and sane whilst having the time of your life. One of the other huge benefits is that you can cover your daily or weekly overheads in just a couple of hours enabling you to train, volunteer, relax or engage in other work or hobby areas as suits. I get asked for tips all the time and have long since thought this massive 'industry' and 'lifestyle choice' needs its own go to manual produced by someone who has been there & bought the T-shirt. Hopefully you will gain invaluable information reading about my mistakes, successes and hard lessons learnt, gather endless useful tips and have a lot of fun whilst entering the fantastic world of 'life on the game' whilst reading the pages of this book.

ABOUT THE AUTHOR

I have been in the adult industry for over 30 years and throughout that time as a successful model, actor, director, producer and Jounalist with a multitude of published work I have continually escorted. I can think of no other job that can make you as much money quickly and repeatedly as the latter but the key is not to let it take-over your life and lead you into a dark place or mind set. Personally, even though I have occasionally had bad, difficult or hugely problematic clients these are very much in the minority and the OK, good and great ones are way over 95% to date so have faith and back yourself to the hilt. In the Internationally recognized World Escort Awards creatively called 'The Hookies' I was 6 times a nominated finalist for 'Best International Escort Of The Year' and a winner more than Once of the Best Escort of that year in my homeland of the UK. As a porn star I have appeared in over 200 movies for a multitude of studios shooting scenes across 4 Continents winning performer of the year and film of the year. I became a model/director for American studio Dickwadd before moving on to running TreasureIslandMedia Europe for 7 years and then continued behind the camera owning and running studios right through to the present day. Along the way I have added numerous awards and titles including Director Of The Year,

Producer Of The Year and even 'Lifetime Achievement Awards'.

I have been a writer and journalist for 15 years with thousands of features published Internationally across 15 separate well-known titles. I am also very ubiquitous across the fetish scene winning Mr Leather UK amongst other accolades and regularly run International fetish events including the annual World Fetish Awards for which I am fortunate enough to be the Chairman. You see what i mean about this being an industry and also possibly a career choice where other doors will open up as all these factors and add-ons greatly feed in to an escorts appeal, visibility and business model and makes him more interesting to clients than say others advertising alongside. I am based in London and it helps for escorting purposes if you are in a location where there is a lot of people, tourists, business men or folks passing through....that said it is possible to escort successfully in my view from any town, village, location in the World....as I bet you will not be the first in your area to do so. Over the last 30 years i have been booked all over Europe, North America, Asia, Australia, South and North Africa and many times in the Middle East (which we will come too later)....South America is still on my to do list but i know of plenty of escorts down there doing great things. The basics apply in whatever territory or time zone you live. Most of all I have enjoyed every minute of it and in the business I am jokingly known as 'The Happy Hooker' & can proudly say it is a fantastic thing to do, be involved in and hopefully it will be for you too.

I would like to offer my personal gratitude to all the hard-working escorts that have contributed to this book. I have asked a number of my colleagues who are well known Internationally in the adult industry to share their short stories of their funniest, worst or most memorable escort experiences between some chapters as a break which i hope you will find enjoyable and educational. I off course cannot thank them enough for their time and candor in passing on their stories. They like myself are all available on social media if you wish to contact any of us as I can assure every one of you they, like most at the top of the industry are great friendly massively professional individuals who I love........but rarely can afford!!!!

CHAPTER INDEX

1 THE INDUSTRY
IN BULLET POINTS

42 Million - The lowest estimate of sex workers in the World today - with no accurate figures for the Middle East and Asia this is likely to be nearer 60 Million (Or about like saying the entire population of the United Kingdom are sex workers).

4% - The number of sex workers that are underage (in their country)

100 Billion - The earnings of sex workers per year.

5 Years - the average career of a sex worker. Very few have long careers and many don't last a month when the phone does not actually ring.

Sex Worker - is the preferred term as most others have some derogatory or dated aspect to them. An issue is that term also includes erotic dancers, Gogo's, adult film actors and online performers MANY of which do not sell contact sexual experiences.

Other well-known terms are:-

Street walker - a sex worker that advertises on the street who will then do sex acts in a car or cheap hotel. Also, very similar to a 'call girl'.

Hooker - North American in particular New York.

Gigolo - A man who sells sex and company to women (See Richard Gere's filmography).

Hustlers and Rent boys - Gay escorts.

Pimp - someone that controls one or more sex workers.

Madam - A female pimp.

Brothel - Where there are a number of sex workers (colloquially a whorehouse but nowadays the word whore always has negative connotations). Used to be called a cathouse but other places you can buy sex are many some but not all Massage Parlours and in Asia barber shops/hairdressers.

Clients - Are known as Johns or Tricks in The Americas and 'Punters' everywhere else.

Escort - The favoured term by all male sex workers and many female as it indicates company rather than the sleazier side of the sex trade.

There are many other great names for sex workers in various regions such as 'Horse Jockey' in Cuba and a Sanky Panky in South East Asia, Sugar Mamas or Janes are rich women who usually keep one younger man or woman (effectively financially rather than an hourly rate. The Man on man equivalent is called a Sugar Daddy with the male sex worker being called a kept boy or boy toy (regardless of his age).

40% - Is the number of prostitutes and male escorts in countries like Cambodia and Thailand which are huge sex tourism destinations.

India has 1.2 Million children which are prostitutes or male escorts (Thailand is very similarly high)

GREEN - is the colour to indicate a male escort according to the legendary hanky code. If worn on the left he is a top and if on the right he is a bottom.

The number of rapes that took place in Netherlands, where prostitution is legal in 2010 is 9.2 per 100,000 population, while in india More than 34,000 cases of rape were reported in 2015 an Average of 6 rapes, 15 molestations each day (Of course there are also Cultural issues in India).

According to International sex worker websites the cities with the most escorts are in order:-

5 Los Angeles

4 London

3 Bangkok

2 New York

1 Beijing

THE TOP 10 COUNTRIES WHERE MEN HAVE PAID FOR SEX AT LEAST ONCE.

10 France 16%

9 Switzerland 19%

8 China 20%

7 USA 21%

6 Netherlands 22%

5 Japan 38%

4 Spain 39%

3 Italy 45%

2 Thailand 75%

1 Cambodia 80%

(Thanks to ProCon.org).

It seems that guys (and it is by far most often men) in the West are much more reluctant to admit they have paid for sex than elsewhere and it is almost certainly the case that their figures in truth are much higher.

2 A BRIEF HISTORICAL TIMELINE OF ESCORTING/ PROSTITUTION

As far back as records exist it seems that escorting and prostitution existed. It seems the earliest recognized record was in 18BC in Mesopotamia where there was official protection of prostitute's rights.

It appears that very generally right through ancient times that prostitution was acceptable, protected and even respected. This changed almost entirely due to one of the World's biggest problems....organised religion. As particularly with the expansion of Christianity and Islam around the globe (plus others) with their enforced moral codes and grandstanding with how someone should live their lives based entirely on often nowadays discredited writings we were told what was acceptable or not, what was good and what was bad. Sex became something to be ashamed off, hidden and taboo along with the naked human body. It is this trend of original acceptability followed by a lengthy period of moral indignation culminating in a more balanced almost open view over the last Century which dominates the entire history of prostitution. Very roughly over the last 2000 years 'The Game' was legal, then became illegal and looked down on and more recently some countries have legalised whereas others are somewhat behind with 'Medieval' wrong century type views.

First Century AD - Ancient Rome was in its prime and all forms of male and female prostitution was legal and licensed. Anyone could visit a working guy or girl without any problems or stigma. Brothels were plentiful and hugely popular and profitable.

2nd Century - Also Ancient Greek culture as we know it was in its heyday and it was identical to that of the Roman Empire as regards 'The Game'. Many prostitutes of the era and the next 500 years were very famous personalities. There were also a large amount of slaves put into prostitution but this was not that bad of a life. Male prostitutes for men was a huge business especially in the army whilst child prostitution run by 'prostitute farmers' was absolutely rampant.

3rd Century - Brothel coins became a thing particularly in territories ruled by the Romans. Many of these have been discovered by archaeologists and they depict every type of sex act you can imagine. They were used both to advertise the price of certain sex acts as well as in some places they were taken as payment rather than money. They also contained pictures of cocks or vaginas with add-ons like wings which meant that escort was particularly well endowed. Various versions of these coins were in use right into the middle ages.

4th Century - Although legal in Ancient Greece prostitution did carry some social stigma but they were very much a necessity and part of every cities culture. At the time sex with slaves was deemed unacceptable which left the door open for the legit selling of sex by the middle and lower class. With guys they tended to be adolescents and could trade until they grew a beard. Afterwards they could become the first ever 'kept boys' but this was secretive as this was socially unacceptable for both parties from early twenties onwards.

5th Century - When the Romans left France Theodoric the Visigoth persecuted pimps rather than the sex workers and the punishment was death....this was a huge 180 turn from the previous liberal Roman period. The following Century his grandson made the job entirely illegal with floggings for both the customer and the escort.

6th Century - The idea of concubines became predominant. They were classed as company almost always sexual where a full marriage was not possible or indeed just for fun. It was hugely popular across the Arabic world where harems were extensive. A Harem referred to a group rather than a place. Concubines were also used extensively to produce a family. It is little known but many men were concubines largely for sexual gratification.

7th Century - The prophet Mohammed declared the selling of sex as forbidden and classed it in Islam as a sin. This like in all other periods of history did not stop it as it mutated into 'sexual slavery' which was not considered prostitution and this became very common.

8th Century - Geishas began to come to the fore in Japan. Often seen as sex workers this is largely not the case and certainly not in modern culture. They were entertainers mainly dancing, singing and performing together with originally but not always some limited sexual services.

9th Century - The Vikings were in their prime and were travelling with their culture far and wide including North America well before Christopher Columbus set foot there. Sex was a very masculine thing to them where women were not so much as second class as about 5th class. Homosexuality was rife as they believed that imbibing & drinking semen was good for muscle growth as well as dominating another guy in the most obvious way, showed power and strength. This was highlighted in the infamous 'Rope game' where men stood either side of a rope before fighting each other with wooden weapons and the losers would become submissive sexually and other ways including being 'followers' into battle. Prostitution did not really exist as money did not change hands as it was generally more 'rape and pillage'.

10th Century - The time of the 'Dark Ages' was when sex work started to get structured and proliferated absolutely everywhere. We had tavern girls, the first brothels, endless street walkers and everything else. To distinguish them from other folk they wore yellow which for a time became the sex worker associated colour. Strangest of all they regularly plied their trade in churches as this was one of the places men gathered and sexual acts were held both on and off the premises with both the congregation and clergy alike.

11th Century - The Turkish bath moved out of its home locality because the Seljuk Empire conquered much of the Byzantine Empire. They were built in every City across Europe, Asia and Africa taking an 'organised' sex trade with it. This was the start of the large mixture of cultures which would dominate the next Millenium.

12th Century - This was the tail end of the crusades and there were just as many women and young guys plying the sex trade following the armies off to war as soldiers. In the First crusade where an army needed washer women, cooks, cleaners etc it was stipulated only ugly women were allowed. This was to stop the men having sexual thoughts and being distracted from their religious endeavours which of course was what the crusades were all about. By the time of the subsequent crusades the sex workers and indeed the soldiers had different ideas and huge numbers of attractive women and young boys went. If a battle was won they were not involved in any celebration but if it was lost they were wholly blamed as a distraction from the moral high road.

13th Century - Prostitutes were made saints this is before religion became puritanical. The most famous of which was Mary Magdalene (Jesus Christ's mother) who was a prostitute according to many accounts but she reformed. religion knew they could not banish the industry so went with the repenting scenario heavily.

14th Century - To protect prostitutes and continue their reform Magdalene Homes named after Mary herself were established by the church often run by very strict nuns. These continued through to the 19th Century where they were known as Magdalene Laundries or sometimes Magdalene Asylums. In the 14th Century the Church again accepting it could not win against prostitution but decided that this route was "the lesser of two evils".

15th Century - and throughout the Middle Ages prostitution had one good thing going for it in that it seemed to be the best prevention to stop rape of non-prostitute men and women. Married men, military guys, sailors and the clergy were particularly horny for new quickie partners and a working girl/guy was the answer. Although they were not respected it was an industry that was tolerated. We also saw the rise of the brothel again for safety of the workers and convenience as much as anything and also red-light districts sprung up in cities. It is thought the term red light came from the coloured lamps the girls used at harbours when ships returned home.

16th Century - Attitudes hardened against the trade due to a massive increase in sexual transmitted disease especially syphilis which for convenience were blamed on brothels and prostitution. This correlation and timing probably had more to do with the knowledge and visibility of STI's than any actual sudden surge. The consequence was that the industry was associated with plague and disease resulting in brothels being outlawed.

17th Century - Branding became in vogue at this time. Prostitutes both male and female were branded with a letter or mark as a punishment for their crime. Often the hot branding iron would be used near the vaginal lips or groin area but other parts of the body were used too. Furthermore, this process was used to show ownership by pimps, an individual or gangs etc. They have Four purposes in that they are humiliating, punishing, psychologically submissive and a sign to one and all. Popular branded letters usually on the arm for criminals are A for adultery, B for Burglary, F for Forgery and T for Thief.

18th Century - Male prostitution in the States became a noticeable thing although there was no structured legislation. This was the big sea going era worldwide and prostitution moved from rural areas to ports where it stayed heavily through to the last Century. Places like Singapore, The Chinese Coastal cities, Portsmouth, London, New Orleans and New York became massive centres of prostitution with major well known brothel districts of 'sex workers' as it was then first called. Sex workers also started using the first ever condoms made from catgut or the bowel of a cow.

19th Century - The traditional 'home' of transaction sex the Turkish bath house moved out of the Middle East again as the new 'Victorian Bath Houses' became hugely popular. This of course then spread through the dominant British Empire around the globe. Authorities introduced a number of legal rules such as the infamous 'Contagious diseases Act' together with an extensive range of new regulations. According to one report 1 in 60 properties in Western Europe was a brothel.

20th Century - Brings us in to the modern era. Communism became a thing and was strongly opposed to the business. In the United States it became illegal between 1910-1915 before becoming legal again and then switching back to its current situation of legality in the odd state but not in the greatest majority. Gay rights started blooming through the 60's and 70's around the likes of Stonewall and the first Pride marches and celebrations which bought sexual freedoms and mind sets that greatly aided the growth of 'The Trade'. The HIV sexual pandemic starting in 1980 was an awful backward step but the genie was out of the bottle and sexual activity would only increase culminating in the arrival of sexual tourism to countries like Thailand and Mexico or some third world destinations. The heyday of street sex. Child prostitution hit the public consciousness and a new term 'Survival sex' was introduced for those that do sex to get food.

21st Century - The internet made marketing for an escort so much easier and many sites grew up (and indeed magazines) to aid this. Probably the most famous and successful of all was Rentboy.com which was a great safe place for working guys to ply their trade until it was raided by the Feds in 2015. Cybersex, Cam sex and fansites like Only Fans became extended and safer ways that adult entertainers could make money. Sex was for sale anywhere and everywhere including the problematic Middle east where Dubai and Israel became massive hubs for the industry in that part of the World. The first proper sex workers Union was formed. There was also the rise in awareness of human trafficking which has gone on since time immemorable.....according to some official figures 79% of trafficking nowadays is sex trafficking including many minors. In 2014 The 'Swedish Model' came into being which criminalised the customer rather than the escort - Amnesty International favour 'The Nordic Model' which exists to make it entirely legal for both parties.

3 ESCORTING IS FOR EVERYONE WHO FANCIES IT

As we have established the sex trade industry is wholly ambidextrous and is populated as much by guys as women. All this writers personal experience is from the gay male to male spectrum but I do know loads of female escorts servicing men and of course those which are happy to be employed with either sex. I hope that much of the general information here although written from my perspective, knowledge and experiences will be equally useful to women, bisexual, straight male or trans escorts in many ways. That said there is some fundamental differences between the situation that male escorts have than female ones.

In the modern era escorts and sex workers have generally faced puritanical views and societal disgust or disapproval. this has meant that many who work in the industry are secretive about their job or part-time job. The use of 'professional names' is standard which is there to be sexy but more importantly to maintain anonymity from friends, relatives and acquaintances old and new. So, it has often been a clandestine industry although becoming less so with increasing gradual social acceptance.

Since time immemorial there has been a very unfair attitude in sex to that of men and women. A man who sleeps around a lot and has many sexual partners whether women or other men is always seen as a stud, stallion, player etc. and is admired or envied by a majority and he if not married will probably be very public about it....boasting of his many conquests in number terms. Women who have many partners are seen exactly in the opposite way as 'whores', 'easy', 'sluts', 'slags' and much worse and are not seen as 'the marrying kind'. Consequently, women will play down their sexual activity so as not to get a 'reputation'. This is unfair but is very much the fact in modern times as well as history and it is this general attitude which is the umbrella difference between the two types of sex worker that effects their marketing, public persona, discretion and so much more.

Male gay escorts are seen as the elite of the queer world along with porn stars and more often than not those two careers come hand in hand......similar with top female models. As the ultimate industry legend Jeff Stryker once told me you can sell sex if you have a great face, body, look and large dick in which case you are highly sort after and almost worshipped. His follow up line was all are great but if you have any two you can make it in the adult business. Gay escorts are seen as experienced, fun, great guys and are looked up too as princes or Lords amongst men. Their trade is not seen as sleazy or degrading in any way. Their clients are not seen as and do not feel like they are doing something seedy or socially embarrassing and it is possibly likely that any gay man would hire an escort if they had the cash as it is not a sign of 'desperation' or similar and it is more just about fun and convenience. Nobody will get pregnant, attached or emotionally involved so it may feel more like a trip to the dentist or barber. There is no stigma to being a gay escort or his client whatsoever and it is almost always the opposite. The only real issue is the publics and guys partaking's acceptance and feelings towards homosexuality, being queer, the closet, outed etc.

Women on the other hand have to come off the back of two millennia of the word 'prostitute', 'whore' 'scarlet woman' or whatever. Basically, through the ages with a handful of exceptions female sex workers are seen as the lowest of the low often not protected legally, shunned by family and friends and treated as fifth rate citizens or some such. if you sell your body you are 'dirty' and should live in shame... With male clients of female sex workers phrases like 'i don't have to pay for sex yet' etc. coming from the ingrained opinion that any man who pays for companionship with a woman is 'desperate', cannot get a shag any other way, one of the dirty mac brigade etc. The end result it seems from my male viewpoint maybe incorrectly that there is a massive amount of stigma in the straight trade attached just as much to those that service it as their customers. This also is extended by the legal attitude to the subject. There is not a lot of good to say about this imbalance except that as many women are making some decent cash that it will become increasingly respected as it should be. Trans escorting is big business but cannot escape from the overarching umbrella of the above pro or negative stigma depending on which way the transition is and how it is perceived rightly or wrongly in society. In a perfect world all sex workers should have no worries like the gay male escorts but it is unfortunate that we do not live in a sterile bubble of universal morals and perceived public opinions. Thank goodness through cam sites and fansites there is now a burgeoning group of very successful women making small fortunes and therefore much of the mentality from say the 1960's/70's and 80's will if not already, disappear.

Men who sell to women are a very small minority indeed which is another great shame. It seems and I am generalizing like crazy here that women are after romance, a boyfriend a life partner/husband......a fairy-tale rather than wham, bam thankyou man anonymous sex. Not helped by the historical fact that man the provider has always controlled the purse strings and until the last couple of decades women have had less access. Basically, if a woman is horny and wants a quickie then not many men will turn them down and that coupled with their desire for some form of 'relationship' means that there is very little overall demand for male escorts servicing women. It is basic supply and demand. The guys i know who provide that service say they can go up to a month without getting an inquiry. As women nowadays have much more income and great jobs than in the past presumably the gigolo/ sex as a convenience business or 'boyfriend experience' will grow exponentially.

The media has not helped as in the past they have tended to show sex workers as unhappy, wounded, scarred individuals like say in Midnight Cowboy, Leaving Las

Vegas, Pretty Baby or My Own Private Idaho and the occasional unbelievable positive fairy story of say Julia Roberts in Pretty Woman is an exception. So many times sex workers are seen as victims, troubled and that image has been perpetrated long enough that it is ingrained. It would be nice to have realistic representation unlike say Richard Gere in American Gigolo or God help us..... Deuce Bigalow: Male Gigolo!

4 LEGALITY

Let's start with a generalization - Selling sex is pretty universally illegal, selling your time is not at all (See accountants/Solicitors/Therapists etc) and there is so much grey area in-between - one common thread is that it tends to be so far down the police's list of priorities that it is largely passed over and ignored unless it becomes problematic. The legality varies from country to country and very often from region to region within a particular nation's borders. Also, to complicate the issue further for both sides there is Four areas of potential criminality -

1   Selling sex
2   Buying sex
3   Organising sex work in any way
4   Solicitiation.

Escorting is legal in some territories and not others so as a basic starting point you should at least know the situation in your country. That said there are a few industry standards which exist to better and poorer degree across the board beginning with the much used 'disclaimer':-

"I do not accept money for sexual acts. I am compensated via contributions for my time only. Anything that happens during that time is a decision made between two consenting adults". (Or something similar).

This is a very basic sentence and there are many versions of this as stars in the heavens with some indicating the service supplied is more to do with health, experience, a sex guru or therapist etc. The basic idea is that in territories where escorting is effectively illegal to have something to protect you somewhat. There are no magic words which make an illegal act suddenly legal so escorts are in a grey area but a clause like this can only help yet is far from watertight or a guaranteed protection to being charged......furthermore it can lead an escort to be complacent about any 'illegal' acts he is going to conduct. Purely and simply there is no pure total get out of jail card to be honest.

Without question the cops the world over are not massively interested in escorts and people selling sexual services compared to their other priorities. A few decades back when the industry was much more on the streets and cards in phone boxes there was a bigger problem of certain areas and locations getting bad reputations or being seen as unsafe or indeed visible to minors and children. Nowadays it is almost all online and the police have much bigger and serious issues to deal with than 2 consenting adults having sex in someone's house or hotel room in exchange for some cash for their time. As a former police officer myself who still knows many guys wearing the badge it seems that it is an incredibly low priority and almost a waste of their time rightly or wrongly as it is unstoppable and any penalties (usually always just small fines) will never deter anyone. So, we have a 'crime' with no real victims, nowadays causing no problems, that will just take up time, cause paperwork, stretch police budgets and achieve nothing therefore almost always sex work 'in reality' goes unpoliced which is great.

This above very much applies to the middle/high end escorts who will probably work for 20/30 years without any legal issues, warnings or arrests nowadays with luck. It is well-known though that mostly when escorts get arrested it is for something else like drug dealing, drug possession, stealing, tax evasion or aggro and then a minor escorting charge will go on top of the other more serious and more heavily policed crimes. My experience and the millions of escorts i know invariably have no problems nowadays unlike say the street arrests for solicitation and the Police stings from the 80's & 90's and before...it is now a much more straight forward safer time thank goodness. Where the authorities do concentrate and rightly so is the areas of sex trafficking, sex slavery and that of minors or any area where someone is forced into the sex industry by others and this book is not aimed at anyone in that world at all. In fact, there are many cases of Middle/High End escorts tipping off authorities to help those forced into the trade so escorts are rapidly getting a good and acceptable image which can only lead one day to full legalisation everywhere. Often there are police officers who specifically are appointed to liase with the industry to keep any of the bad practices at bay. If anyone reading this is being forced into sex work against their will then contact me through ay means at your disposal and i will do my best to get thhe right authorities and best help for you i can.

For the time being the situation remains that selling your time is not a crime whether you are a psychologist, fitness instructor, yoga teacher or indeed an escort providing company. Escorts will have clients who just want a dinner or travel companion without any sex acts provided and this is the backbone of our protection to carry on what we do as obviously this is 100% legal...... if you fancy each other and get down and dirty then where is the problem. The best tip one can give is too not discuss sex acts with clients (which may not be easy) and not to take money up front instead getting paid at the end which looks much better legally and of course in the million to one chance your client is an undercover cop it will not get that far. That said payment at the start or end we will come to later as there are other pros and cons with both.

SO, WHERE IS THE SEX TRADE LEGAL OR NOT?

There are Five rough groups and these should be crossed with the Four areas above (Buying/Selling/Organising and Soliciting) making 20 variants in all but it's basically as follows

A LEGAL/DECRIMINALISED for buyers/sellers/ organisers and soliciting - Including such major territories as New Zealand, Most of Australia and parts of Africa.

B PART LEGALISED where sex work is accepted and legalised - Such as Germany, Austria, Hungary, Netherlands, Turkey, The rest of Australia and many countries in South & Latin America.

C   ABOLITIONISM where selling and buying sex is not illegal but the organising and soliciting of it is - such as in UK, Italy, Spain, Poland, Belgium, Finland, Denmark, Czech Republic, India, Malaysia, Most of the Caribbean, Brazil, the rest of Central America, the rest of Africa except the strong Muslin countries.

D   NEO-ABOLITIONISM 'THE SWEDISH MODEL' - Where the only illegality is on the buyer and the sex workers are supposedly all acting legally - such as Canada, France, Sweden, Norway, Iceland, Ireland & Israel.

THEN WE HAVE THE COUNTRIES STUCK IN THE WRONG CENTURY ON THIS:-

E PROHIBITED/ILLEGAL Where sex workers, buyers, those that organise and solicit are all deemed to be criminals (although the enforcement and policing varies hugely) - Here we have 95% of the USA, All the Middle East and strong Muslim countries, Russia and China of course and a bunch of smaller uninteresting backward looking countries where most decent sex workers would not be interested in visiting anyway and cash or clients are not plentiful.

5 ESCORT TALES -
DALLAS STEELE

My Most Unusual Escorting Experience

He flew me first class from Dallas to one of the big gambling cities in Nevada. When I walked out of the terminal, the uniformed driver was waiting with my name on his sign. We headed twenty miles out of town into the dry, barren desert of the Silver State, then another six miles off-road in the big Cadillac Escalade.

The house was a massive three-story log-cabin looking structure. Not another house anywhere in sight. I looked at my phone. No cellular service either. The driver dropped me off with a cautionary "good luck."

The door opened to reveal a man in his seventies and seven-foot-tall bronze statue of a firefighter in the center of the living room. Off to the side was an elegant shrine of candles and pictures, all of them of an attractive man who appeared to be in his forties.

"He was my David. He was a firefighter who I hired as my escort and boyfriend for 11 years," my host said. "He got cancer by breathing chemicals in a fire.

But instead of treatment, he blew his brains out here in the living room two months ago." He gestured to the bloodstains on the floor.

"You remind me so much of my David. Can I call you by his name for the weekend? And I'd be really honored if you'd wear his clothes I laid out on the bed," he went on.

I took a very deep breath. If I refused, where would I go? I would surely die in the desert, so I decided to play along.

He was incredibly eccentric and wealthy. We went to dinner at a casino where post meal, he gambled around $12,000 in four hours and gave me $2000 to gamble with. We got home and he asked me to top him as he inhaled poppers face down. The request came with a caveat. He said he had a heart problem and if anything happened, to call the number on the nightstand. I wasn't to say anything, just call it, then start walking into the desert. He said someone would pick me up. Quite reassuring.

During sex, every time I came or pretended to, he would flip over, whip out a $100 bill and wrap it around my equipment. We'd still be asleep by 10pm, but he'd get up at 3am and go back to the casino, gambling for two more hours, then wake me up at six for more sex.

The money was very good for a weekend, usually $5000, sometimes more. I once told him about my credit card debt. He offered to pay off all $28,000, but

I balked it was too much. He asked what would be good. I said I could always use $10k. The next morning, there was a check on the nightstand for $10,000. When he talked about going on a cruise with his wife and adult children back east, he meant they spend $250,000 and charter a yacht for a week.

I saw him five more times until he emailed me to say he had chosen a boyfriend among the three escorts he'd been seeing. I had no idea I was on a reality show where I could be eliminated. He said the "winner," was a single guy who didn't do porn and was a Republican Trump supporter (as he was). He planned to continue seeing me just for sex, but the other escort said he could have only him.

Over the course of my time seeing him, I more than paid off all of my credit card debt, but it was hard work pretending to be someone else for someone who really needed to get some help with his loss.

6 WHO CAN BE AN ESCORT?

The transaction of sex for money or company relies on Two parties. Does the escort have something worth selling and does the customer have enough free money for a good time. Everyone has a dick and ass and with so many offering sex for free who is actually paying for it. The simple answer is that you are getting a service for your money when you want it, with the guy you want doing exactly what you want and not doing stuff that does not interest you or turns you off.....it is a service of convenience exchanged for money.

Therefore, do you have something to offer? Are you as fit as fuck? do you have a great face, body or ass? Do you have a massive cock etc. IF you are 'average' and describe yourself as such then your phone will simply not ring. Escorts spend a huge proportion of their time in the gym as their body is their business and likewise, they will eat well and look after themselves generally. That said guys get hired for all sorts of reasons from big feet to tattoos, or piercings etc. as long as they are above the norm or have that one thing of interest to others. It is not all about physical looks as some of the most successful escorts are those that offer specific services and these are as many and varied as stars in the sky. You can have massive balls, be a fisting top, an aggressive master, have a large sex toy collection, a sling, some uniform or other, like getting pissed over and on and on it goes. Your job or past occupation may also help if applicable - there are very successful ex-military guys, ex-pro sportsmen, current truckers, builders, mechanics etc. who are extremely busy escorts selling a real-life sexual fantasy service. What does not work is 'i am a normal guy, with an average body, average cock not offering anything special' - you should target your customers, get them excited or interested and ringing you not any of the other 20 guys in adverts alongside yours.

Nationality also works as some customers will be looking for an Asian escort, Latino, Brit, yank, Aussie, dirty German, blonde Swede, hunky hung black guy, sexy little Brazilian etc they all work...it is just about making yourself as interesting in a 'sexy' way as possible. Occasionally read some of the other escort's adverts and you will see how little thought and effort they put into it and you can be assured they are hugely unsuccessful in gaining work. One of the biggest aids to success of all is if you do or have done adult film work. Porn stars are seen as elite, experts, hot as hell and are the most sort after escorts by far and this can be reflected in the price they charge and rightly so. They are seen as glamourous, fantasy figures presumably previously wanked over many times, they are perceived as the stars of sex, will be the best shags but also the anticipation and excitement will be there as well as bragging rights after the event. As there is only one say Dolf Dietrich, Brent Corrigan or Francois Sagat then if you want them as a fan and only them then the price asked will be reflected. Many of the leading porn stars are charging and able to get many, many thousands of dollars per night...if you have got it flaunt it, sell it and cash it up.

All ages, body types, skin colour, nationalities, orientations, transitions can and do escorting successfully but there are many of each type who are equally as unsuccessful and the job of this book is to make you the former rather than the latter.

My own escorting career has gone through many cycles. When I first left the military I was so concerned about bringing my regiment into disrepute that I did not mention my previous job. Likewise, my short time as a cop also stayed out of my descriptions. The irrational fear was that I would end up in the newspapers under some headline about all taxpayers hard earned money went into training a sex worker. After a year I concluded that I was not that interesting to the media nor likely to be (well until a few years later when certain celebrities came into the equation) and so I marketed the hell out of my two previous jobs. It not only worked but it exploded, my phone was ringing on repeat and I barely had time to pull my pants up before they were dropped again for the next punter who it seemed was interested in some hot butt sex with a real-life soldier or cop. I then went and got some specific pictures done at photo shoots I organised myself and within a few months I was one of the World's leading escorts with a busy 'dance card' and being flown all over the place just to nut in a guy. At the same time whilst I was doing some club and personal security work (which when mentioned in advertising too also helped greatly with bookings) the adult porn industry noticed me and I did my first scene with an International studio called Eurocreme and as soon as that was released and publicised yet more escort bookings resulted - so i did some more filming and got even busier and on and on it goes.

As mentioned above age is not a problem in the escort World. OK the average age is mid-twenties but that is not a problem whatsoever. I did my first client at 37yo and have had MANY bookings right through the next two decades. The oldest escort currently working successfully is in his late Seventies. The key is to accept who you are and sell accordingly. A 60-year-old cannot compete with a 21-year-old probably on the basics but if he is selling himself as experienced, masculine, more interesting company, a daddy, bear, fetish guy or whatever then he will always be busy. Not everyone wants to hire 21yo's anyway so why compete with them. if you are a twink then work that market and image hard - you will probably be booked on your youthful good looks alone. 10 years later if you are still selling just on looks then you will lose out heavily to the newest twinks on the block, yet if you grow some facial hair and move into the more masculine markets then you will be as busy as any twink out there. Likewise 10 years further on use the word daddy on your profile, wear some leather or offer some specific sex acts that you like, maybe fisting, BDSM, foot fucking, watersports, master/slave (the sort of things twinks never offer and even if they do it does not sit right on them and their lack of experience and equipment will soon let them down). The result is you, if wise will always have something which is marketable unless you stand still in which case old father time will steadily erode your business and your regulars will move on..... as they always will do. Escorts are businessmen and the best escorts are great businessmen indeed who know themselves well, what they have that others do not have and likewise their own limitations but most of all how to interest their customers old and new.

WHAT THE CLIENT IS LOOKING FOR?

One of the main reasons a customer hires a guy is for convenience. Nowadays free apps and online hook-up sites are full of 'timewasters' who talk, suddenly go quiet, never meet up or have no actual intention of meeting up. If you hire an escort you will get the guy of your choice at a time that suits you staying for as long as you want doing what you want rather than what his choice or interests maybe. This could be fitting in with a lunch break, in a strange town, on business, when you have returned from the pub, club etc. or whenever you are horny, high or in need of sex. One call and you are all sorted. Hook-up Apps are time hoovers whereas escorts are all about convenience....if you can afford one.

There are so many reasons why someone hires an escort from company for dinner in a new town maybe with a little play afterwards right through to being central to a 'party' where you may be hanging with a number of guests, the centre of attention or putting on a bit of a show or performance. Other popular reasons will be guys are having a bit of a chem session and no-one can get hard or cum so time to call in a professional. Or guys often want to experiment with something a bit more extreme, out of the ordinary or purely something their actual partner won't do or is not interested in. Furthermore, straight guys, bi-curious and those shy and wanting to lose their virginity find hiring over the phone is the easiest, less stressful or worrying way of doing this. Escorts tend to have the highest cherry taking count amongst their peers by a massive margin. So, basically a customer is looking for company, convenience, experience or is just plain horny, shy or nervous but usually it is all of those together in some form and when an escort works that out he can do a much better job at attracting, satisfying and getting repeat clients and having fun whilst doing it and earning also. In all business transactions the perfect deal is when both sides feel as though they have what they want rather than some large imbalance on one side or the other.

Power is a useful thing to consider in sex work as in which side has it and the real answer is both. The client has cash which the sex worker wants and he can control who he employs, for how long and what happens during said agreed time. On the other hand the sex worker is almost always the more experienced and most relaxed of the two and invariably takes the lead and offers or suggests different things to try and in what order or how the session progresses. Of course, often the client wants to be dominated, fucked or in the hands of someone in charge and this is an interesting dynamic as he has the money power whereas he wants the escort to be in control totally when together. It is this underlying scenario which over time has led to the 'cash is on the side table' scenario moving the money away mentally from the meet. The session will not be happening without money being exchanged yet the actual physical payment process is the least sexy and most undermining part in many ways of your time together. Of course, sometimes a customer just wants a 'boyfriend experience' and again the further away the money transaction is kept the better for all. Nowadays with online banking, hand held card machines, PayPal etc. a lot of transactions are done completely before the meet or with regulars well after the meet a million miles away from the actual physical company or sex part.

There are Three reasons why a client picks one escort over another for the first time

1   Pictures
2   His name
3   The activity or niche required.

1   Pictures. This seems pretty obvious from the longstanding cliche we all know off 'A Picture is worth a Thousand words'. Away from the escort industry in the standard world of hook up sites and hook up apps there are many stats but they all come in at over 95% better response if you have a picture and the clearer more interesting or explicit (if allowed) the better. When someone is looking for an escort they will go onto a website or some other place and be presented with the choice of hundreds of guys. Almost certainly the 2 or 3 they consider will be chosen wholly on the single picture presented. Where possible upload as many pictures

and as varied as you can on your follow up page. Clearly show the big 5 - a) your face, b) your body c) your cock erect d) your back and e) your ass and of course use relevantly recent pictures and if possible make them interesting with the chosen location or your stance (Maybe outdoors if you can). Maybe use a universally known object like a Coca Cola bottle or remote control alongside your manhood to show size. There are tricks of the trade like do press ups beforehand to make the muscles look bigger, shave your pubic hair to make your cock seem bigger as well as take the shot from below for the same result. An open ass, well displayed is also a great idea. Wear some sexy or fetish gear and consider paying for a professional still shoot as this is in effect your business shop window in one little thumb nail.

2   Escorts Name - If you have been in adult films and have a somewhat recognizable name then use that and only that as it is a big seller. It is one of the biggest reasons to appear in porn where over the last decade the basic wages have diminished a fair bit but the publicity and fantasy value you get from being on film and wanked over worldwide is invaluable to your escort business. Porn stars can always charge more for their time and many clients are happy to pay this for bragging rights of 'i was fucked by Cutler X' or 'I fucked Skyy Knoxx' etc. which they will be talking about to their buddies for many years after the memory of a regular one on one escort with a non-model has long been forgotten. Purely and simply there is only one Rhyheim Shabazz, Allen King, Michael Roman or

Silver Steele and if you are a fan you will spend whatever is asked in price to spend time with them and other guys (maybe fitter/younger/more hung/ closer by) just will not even compete in the clients mind which is heavily laden with hours of fantasy wanks about certain guys on film. I am sure there are much higher figures out there but the highest I have heard off for a nights company with a named 'porn star' is $6000 which could be 10 times what fit hung guys with no particular identity, brand, name, selling point may get for exactly the same time and the same service. In a similar way if you have an interesting job or have had in the past then use this in your name as it will help you stand out from all the other guys. I know of many ex-army guys, current guys in the navy, cops doing a second job, builders, ski instructors, personal trainers, sportsmen that have very enhanced escort businesses pushing the 'reality' fantasy of sleeping with a real marine, fireman, trucker, rugby player etc. and maybe you can have slightly higher rates also or go for a higher number of clients.

3   The Activity or Niche Required - Some clients will be shopping around for something specific away from the route one standard guy to fuck or get fucked by in a hotel room for an hour. If you heavily market this even though you will be possibly miss out on 90% of the middle of the road clients, you will be right at the top of the list of choice by those looking for something in particular. These can range from pitching yourself as the best company and most presentable and educated for a business event, dinner or pretend boyfriend to accompany

for a while through to the extreme areas of services that you like supplying, enjoy or have equipment for. This latter list is basically infinite and for example you may pitch yourself as a foot fetishist or have big or smelly feet, maybe you are into leather, rubber, sportswear or female lingerie. Possibly you want to offer a bondage service, CBT/ BDSM one, a daddy or son situation and on it goes. If you have special equipment (Or clothing like say a cop uniform or a priest's outfit) then mention it. Customers may be looking for sex toy action, fuck machines, milking machines, a guy with corporate punishment equipment & restraints, electro, saline etc. etc. Being ex-military and ex-Police myself this is something I have used very successfully myself. I am also a leatherman and into a lot of extreme sex practices and I push them all and play the niche side of the industry hard and it works.....but only if it is real and genuine so please do not go and pretend to be something you are not or into some practice you have little experience or desire off.

I once did a duo two escort job organised by the client who had used me before and wanted me to top him whilst he was fucking the other guy. When I arrived I knew the other escort and I also knew he was a top. Sure enough all was well until we got down to the serious bit of the session; I did my bit but after 10 seconds the other 'top' escort acting as a sub in effect just for the cash called a halt to proceedings and then announced that he could only take 2 or 3 strokes maximum!. An argument ensued and basically I got paid and was rebooked many times in the future and the other escort got absolutely nothing except a very bad review online. So don't sell or market yourself incorrectly as you will be found out. One of the most successful escorts I ever knew was a German lad who was an ex-professional soccer player of some renown. He used this in his marketing and basically his booking schedule was always full and his phone never stopped going yet he only ever used one pic of him in his footie kit but the reality of bedding him went straight to a thousand horned up client's wallets and everyone was happy on both sides.

Many years ago (and we are talking 20 plus) a magazine called corporal contacts to fill space used my escort advert without my permission or any payment from me. I was happy and did provide CP to clients but it was not the mainstay of my business and yet I did get many calls and still do today asking to just cane, paddle or beat a guy for cash which I have done a number of times and it highlighted to me how potent targeted marketing of your escort service could be but in that case being highly sexed i did those jobs but had no desire to specialize in that. Basically, in escorting niches and targeted markets work and are very good indeed and always better than trying to compete with the thousands of other fit guys with decent dicks which are all interchangeable and merge into one in a client's shopping spree around the middle bland part of the market.

7 WHAT DOES IT TAKE?

There are many different types of successful escort and they all come in various shapes, sizes and from every ethnicity and are offering a varied degree of services. The one deciding factor is that you have to have something a client will pay for. Obviously with smart phone apps and online hook up website's guys can find free sex readily but a lot of these as mentioned earlier are timewasters or have no intention of meeting but will exchange messages for weeks on end, often many of these guys are not to your taste or not offering what you specifically want or at a convenient time. The introduction of a financial transaction short circuits this and speeds the whole situation up and has a guaranteed end result. Yet, the simple fact remains that why should someone pay you for company or sex when others will do it for free.

The answer is of course that you have something worth paying for which could be a fantastic body, massive cock, loads of gear, good/quick availability or be an expert in some area. I had a great regular client who was very fit and I would have loved to have fucked him but what he wanted was to be suspended upside down for long periods and have the soles of his feet beaten and burnt which is technically called Bastinado

(He even bought a copy of the Oscar winning film Midnight Express each time which featured this prominently). The fact was he had a great boyfriend that gave him all the sex he wanted but was not into this act so he came to me and was prepared to pay for the privilege for up to 4 hours !!!...this underlines that he wanted a service which I could offer that he could not find at home and not with hook ups so was more than happy to pay big time for it. It also underlines that even though I would have loved to have had sex with him we did not as that was not what he needed from an escort.....in his case he could get that satisfactorily at home.

Anyone can be an escort - but you must have something. The average lifespan of an escort is about 3 months this is because so many people enter the industry on the basis of 'I am good company', 'I like sex' and 'I am good at sex' without any reference to are they going to be any good at this job or have something to offer a paying customer. They then make endless mistakes (Hence this book) before leaving the industry a few weeks later when their phone is not going or they have a couple of bad experiences...often self-inflicted that could have been avoided. Long-term escorts or career escorts work this out very fast. They have great clear pictures hopefully professionally produced, clever names, descriptions that draw guys in and they invest in themselves, their businesses and brands. Simply they are professionals in the job for the right reason rather than a fast buck. The biggest factor is that they have worked out what makes them different, special or worth hiring and focus on that across the board with a laser like focus. There are many cases of fit guys failing dismally as escorts and equally switched-on guys with possibly less to offer doing well by being focused, clever or putting themselves in the clients' shoes and working backwards.

So, we have these two opposing rules. Basically, if you are fit, have a big dick etc. it is obvious that guys will pay for your company and want remunerated sex likewise everyone else can do the job too if they target and market properly. That said the greatest majority of escorts do not make it long term so do some research, work out your unique USP and work at being successful and raising yourself above the throng. Everything is saleable to someone so if you are black, Asian, have tattoos, piercings, Muslim, have a belly, are handicapped, trans, 60 plus, have huge feet, sweat or fart a lot etc. don't hide that instead make it central to your look, business and presentation - take it from me this way lies lucrative work and repeat business. Just make your business the very best it can be and certainly the best in its individual lane. At all costs stand out.

Your location may also be a major factor. if you are in a big urban city in a rich country then you will be good to go but expect plenty of competition......It is rumoured that there are more Escorts in New York than bagles or taxi cabs. If you live in a rural area or a poorer country you may struggle but at least hopefully your costs will be lower as some consolation. When travelling I have noticed huge differences in where the work is plentiful but my rule of thumb has always been that the best places are wealthy cities with limited gay infrastructure. My busiest 5 have been Athens, Houston, Johannesburg,

Brussels and Washington DC...in fact Washington was always CRAZY busy and my least successful were San Francisco, Sydney, Sitges and Berlin as too much 'free' competition. When you are new to a location or just visiting you benefit from 'fresh blood' syndrome and you should get an initial couple of weeks novelty bump of interest provided you know how to get the word out in different territories as they all have differing ways for clients to find escorts but this is where an element of prior research comes into play. The middle East is huge for escorts (AYOR) where all the above factors feature heavily but of course there are very unique challenges, issues and dangers there from the authorities which is why their escorts tend to advertise as being based in London, Paris, Madrid, Berlin or Tel Aviv sometimes with say Dubai or UAE as their secondary location. In conclusion even if you are the hottest guy on earth but you are based in a small town a couple of hours away from say Rio, Chicago, St Petersburg or Hong Kong then you will struggle and will need regular trips to more lucrative locations in your country or across borders where you can binge earn for a week or two which is a very worthwhile business model to consider.

So, the answer to this chapter is that yes you do have what it takes to be an escort and successful but you have to get it right, work hard on it, be adaptable and have perseverance as entioned above the greatest majority will not succeed and that will not be because of basic phyical factors it is almost always due to the fact they are expecting a free lunch, easy money and with little effort.

8 ADVERTISING & MARKETING

This is such an important chapter and it is an ever-moving situation which is equally getting harder on a yearly basis or easier depending on your viewpoint, location and other factors. As Western society becomes more liberal and accepting with their morals and as legality for escorting improves then you have more avenues for visibility but equally as the internet takes over this industry like most others then we are liable to the vagaries and external decision making processes of faceless companies. These guys can turn on and off your business with just a flick of a switch...for example look at the sudden switching off of adult content overnight by Pornhub in 2020 or Only Fans and X-Tube the following year.

Right through history escorts have existed in brothels or on street corners - both still exist today but in very, very limited ways. We left the street kerbs to enter the world of back page classified ads in general or niche publications. Since then, we have progressed to the mega buck internet websites such as the much-missed Rentboy.com before heading onto phone apps and hook up sites. In the 2020's almost all escorts are self-employed and are responsible for their own brand, businesses and marketing. There is a lot of free marketing avenues available to you and even more advertising paying opportunity's and generally the best results come from a mixture of the two - remember in life you get what you pay for and investing in yourself and improved visibility is investing in your business and will bare fruit.

Escort Agencies

This is rapidly becoming less relevant as due to the World Wide Web guys can and do now market themselves easily and apply whatever levels of security they wish which were the two main reasons for agencies to exist - hence they are becoming largely obsolete. It is a pretty straight forward business model they find the client organise everything and collect the money and send you the fee minus their deducted agency percentage (which will possibly be something like 20-30%). One of the big issues is that there is no direct line of contact between escort and client so often lots of relevant stuff for a great meeting is missed. Agencies tend to be used by the most nervous, shy or closeted/married clients so they have their place but often the client sees a different picture to that of the escort they will eventually meet....and for a much higher rate than if they went directly. In the past agencies have operated from a location with the escorts all there in one place like modern day versions of brothels but this is the area most heavily policed and enforced by law along with pimps. The easier one on one approach, see exact pictures, ask whatever questions you like both ways is a much better model so it is no doubt that direct bookings now dominate. The other big change from brothel/street walking/agency type set-up to the current more direct route is the mobile phone and smartphones which have revolutionised the escort industry alongside the rise of the internet. Agencies will do all the advertising and marketing for you so just turn up and do the jobs they find for you and hopefully you will have a steady stream. Most importantly if the client wants repeat bookings or an extended session do put it all through the agency as going behind their back is the biggest no no and will lead you to being blacklisted by that company and others as they do chat with each other. Be aware that in places like Las Vegas where photo ads are given out in the street that the guy who turns up will not be the guy in the picture and the price agreed is for him meeting you and anything you then want to do is classed as an extra and the negotiations have to start when often clients think that has already been completed.

Magazines and free papers

The traditional way of advertising which if you have a suitable title in your area can be very productive BUT placing adverts this way can be pretty expensive. In the 90's and '00's every major City had free press and its biggest advertisers, once the premium phone line bubble burst was individual escort ads. Guys used them because they worked repeatedly pure and simple and they were effective. As advertising of all sorts moved over to the internet so did much of the escort ad dollar. Magazines have limited reach whereas the internet is much wider if you can get noticed but even more useful is the internet advertising is cheaper and there is much more freedom, no laws and limited regulation. Over time the traditional classified ads in magazines that allowed adult adverts (a huge earner) have diminished in favour of modern technology and there have been a few high profile well publicised landmarks such as the ending of escort ads in the massive Crags List in 2018. This is a sign of the times and unless there is a great magazine title in your area with good distribution and is known or found by vistitors/ travelling business men then there are better methods.

Websites

Now we move onto the main areas where you can make a lot of money escorting and you should be directing your marketing attention towards. There are a number of great websites set up to market escorts and rent boys and they are the go to place for customers the world over. The problem is that no one site works well in every region so you have to do a bit of research as to what works where you are or where you are temporarily travelling too on an escort/filming/holiday trip. There was an amazing much missed company called Rentboy. com owned and ran by the incredible Jeffrey Durant which had phenomenal reach almost everywhere who were unfortunately raided and put out of business in 2015 for non escort reasons. Since then, no one site has fully filled the void and become as useful as the one stop shop for all that Rentboy was. Possibly the one with the widest coverage is the Dutch owned Rentmen.com but as mentioned above in some territories there may be better more well-known local sites that will serve you well. For example, in most of Northern Europe you should be using a site called HUNQZ.com formally known as Gay Romeo but this does not travel to say North America where you will get effectively zero eyes on. So do that research or ask around and you will discover the most utilised in your region such as in the UK it is Sleepyboy.com but this will have next to no clients or indeed escorts once you leave those islands.

These sites may let you post in a limited fashion for free but they exist to make money so offer better positioning, more visibility and full features if you pay the monthly fee (Or weekly/yearly depending). If serious about this line of work these fees are well worth paying and anyway can be claimed back as a business expense. The monthly figure will be somewhere between 10 and 50 dollars which you can make back in 15 minutes with your first client.

The real key for success here is a great picture that represents you and your service in one image to gain a client's scrolling interest and then you can expand more on your longer profile. Also, a killer title or simply your name if you work in the extended adult industry or even better for porn studios. If you are a top show your cock, if a bottom show your ass, if you are a trucker or builder use an outdoor representative image etc. and be aware that those showing clear faces get a MUCH better rate of response.

Apps

Seeing as so many do all their online activity on their smart phones these days there is often little difference to most folks as regards web site and app usage. All of the website brands have switched to phone friendly versions often with GPS location features but of course they have tended to be over taken by bespoke Apps such as Scruff, Grindr, Tinder, BBRT etc. These are effectively hook up sites and not for escorts and in fact escorting is largely forbidden the trouble for escorts nowadays is that guys when horny or travelling are increasingly using a method they are not formally allowed to work on. So, what's to do?.

Escorts tend to use all of these Apps with maybe the exception of Tinder which tends to have drifted into the guise of a place for people looking for long term relationships and partners rather than a more sexual meeting. The key is not to mention escorting anywhere or hint at it including dollar signs or key words and instead use 'professional' looking pictures especially highly sexual ones in the galleries rather than the pinned picture which usually has to be pretty PC. When guys approach you, it is suggested that you send them your phone number and then can reveal you are for rent only politely where they may engage or as is their right move on. This forced subterfuge instilled on us by the conglomerate media companies can annoy some guys understandably who are not interested in hiring so always be polite and apologetic but this is the only way to a major part of the market. Hopefully, increasingly there will be more escort friendly Apps located with companies in territories with friendly legal laws to the trade such as the wonderful Spanish based MachoBB.

Experience has shown that you can be open on some Apps as regards business like Scruff and the Bear Apps where the moderators are busy elsewhere or more lenient whereas with others like Grindr expect to lose your profile periodically at the mere mention of triggers such as a dollar sign or the words escort/trade. In this case you merely delete your suspended account and re-open a new one using a different email address and off you go again... It's an inconvenience but that's the state of affairs and these companies have to protect themselves from being seen as selling sex or promoting prostitution drawing the ever fervent ire of the no-life right wing anti sex, anti-everything lobby who fill their dull lives by going on and on about sex trafficking and sex slavery etc. which of course is bad but not a reason to cancel all sex. The latest addition to most sites is that you can upload a video of yourself and there is also map locators so guys can find escorts nearby. Take a look at the other ad's and see what the guys put to give you ideas and also indicate why you have to rise above the masses and the competition.

Social Media

There is the similar situation on twitter, Facebook, snapchat, Instagram etc as the Apps in that they have rules against escorting so you need to be a bit more candid. They are great at getting your image in front of many potential customers but you cannot be obvious with the business side of things. Facebook is hyper vanilla particularly as regards images and suspensions are plentiful but there are a lot of very frustrated guys on that platform who may be drawn in by your PC images that you can talk around. Twitter and others are a lot more open to very explicit images and this can be used to your advantage but you will have to keep transaction and business discussions to private messages. Social media is best for advertising your (in their eyes) more legal services such as selling used underwear, jocks or condoms, dildo's, bottles of piss or whatever and of course your Only Fans/JustForFans sites which can all make you money and extend your branding which you should be creating around your home escort business.

Porn and Live Appearances

The best advertising of all is to make a name for yourself Internationally which will make you a sort of VIP escort and in the highest demand bracket which will show in increased work, more clients and higher rates per hour than the norm. If you work for a porn studio or a web studio, they will heavily promote you and it is also something you can use extensively in your own marketing. Nothing draws attention from the wide pool of escorts out there than the words 'International Porn Star', your recognizable name alone or the well-known indicator of this world 'XXX'. Live appearances, Gogo and sex shows have exactly the same positive marketing potential. The venues have to sell tickets and are using your name, image, hosting skills or very prescence to do this and will promote the event over and over again across all media and via their extensive databases therefore by default promoting you extensively which you can use to build your branding and extend the most lucrative part which is your escort business. Best of all these forms of advertising will last you a lifetime and you can turn your fans old and new into clients for as long as you want and give them endless bragging rights and stories to tell their mates which will only help your market reach even more. The best way to make big bucks long term is to have a well-known name Internationally and as there is only one of you guys will contact you well in advance of their travel plans to confirm your availability, seek you out wherever and hopefully invite you on business trips and holidays...... they want you and no substitute. These will often be First Class all the way and are great fun as well as being highly lucrative. You could make your current annual salary in just two weeks with the majority of that time being on a beach, by a pool or in a club.

Other methods

Basically, anything you can think of to get your name out there from doing magazine articles to running a blog or getting in with the big bloggers. The ultimate marketing tool has and always will be word of mouth. If you provide a great service clients will recommend you to their mates and tell them things like whenever you are in Chicago you should hire this guy as he is great or very discrete etc. There are endless bad escorts with poor services and business skills who are often crap at sex, being intimate and even interacting with new guys who maybe need relaxing, are nervous or want to expand their horizons. My unofficial view is that a client hires 5 escorts to find 1 who provides him with a great service and what he needs. Therefore when they find such a guy they will talk about it to friends which will greatly peak their interest and gain you new customers who will seek you out and only you as well as get you repeat work (which may often be years apart if a business guy is from an overseas territory but believe you me they will keep hold off your number and details for a return session....). My record with the same client is 9 years with him holding my number and memory all that time. This is particularly noticeable with celebrities and guys who want or need discretion which we will have a whole chapter on later. They often have private little messaging groups and recommend discrete quality escorts across them advertising your name and contact details on your behalf without your knowledge. You will see this particularly with professional sports teams where you get one 'famous sports man' and over the next few months you will find other team members or indeed from opposition teams coming on board as new clients which he has passed on as these guys find it difficult if not impossible to hook up in clubs and be proactive on hook up apps or websites so surreptitiously help their peers out. So far i have had 4 guys from the same top flight professional football club, 5 guys from one rugby club and that is not to mention my record in South Africa with the former national rugby team a few years back but discretion is always your keystone. Every time all the subsequent bookings have come from one initial brand-new client who obviously enjoyed his time with me and took the initiative to pass my details on through his team privately to other guys he knew were similarly looking for under the radar/off the grid quality professional discrete escorts. The real upside with this is that these guys have large amounts of disposable cash and are usually sexually and company undemanding as they do not get the chances to have the larger number of random coitus that us 'civilians' enjoy from the minute we come of age. They also tend to be as fit as fuck, good tippers and you will not believe you are being paid handsomely for having sex with such hotties.

9 ESCORT TALES - HUNGYOUNGBRIT

When i was just starting out escorting all my work came directly from agencies and this was quite a safe way for a young twinky chav guy to work. The trouble is the lack of information and direct contact you get about what a client wants before you meet. I was once working in the States for an agency called Choirboys and they sent me to meet a client in a hotel room and it all sounded pretty straight forward and vanilla. Afterwards, I found out that the guy was heavily into role play and pretty full-on consensual domination and aggro which the agency had omitted to mention to me prior.

At the meet he came on all nasty and aggressive and i genuinely thought he did not like me but it was part of his thing and yet I had no idea. Being a pro i carried on as best i could thinking it's only an hour and i do not want to get a bad reputation or review with my agency. He was flinging me about the room and then slapping my ass and face and he was much larger than me. It was almost half-way through the session that i saw how hard his dick was and how much he was enjoying himself so i mutated into extreme willing sub mode. At the end he was so nice and polite and said what a great time he had had and that when back in town he would book me again. The penny really dropped when he gave me a large tip and said he hoped i did not take too seriously all the mind games stuff. When I checked back in with the agency later on a very unconcerned guy said 'Oh yeah i forgot to mention he wanted to start off at 100 miles per hour in full-on mode and not drop out of character' to which i suggested that sort of information is pretty important for an escort to know actually if for no other reason than his safety. Yet the agency guy seemed uninterested, but the lesson was learnt that when someone else books the job be prepared for anything and that first impressions may be very wide of the mark.

10 YOUR ADVERT

PICTURE - This is by far the most important part of your escort business. You should consider getting professional and staged photos done as this is your shop window. If at all possible show your face clearly as this will greatly increase your business possibilities. No-one wants to hire a headless torso and there is a well-known rule of thumb - if a guy is hiding his face then there is usually a reason for it. If you are a top show your cock and if a bottom show your ass...it's all very obvious but you would be surprised. If you have a big or thick cock take a picture of it by a known sized article like say a coke can or beer bottle.

Many sites will not allow an explicit picture as your main gateway/pinned image so think hard about getting a good clean pic too. No client is ever going to click on you unless they are triggered by your image...alone; fact. Subsequent pictures can usually show what you like, are offering and into and usually more is better but only if they show some different side of you. If you are offering BDSM or CP then pose with some of your equipment, if you are a biker, semi-pro sports guy, soldier, leatherman then use at least some pictures to back this up and draw the customer in. If you are a master then dress accordingly with say reflective sun glasses, cigar, peaked cap etc and likewise if a sub display that pose maybe with your asshole open, wear a chain/dog collar or with a range of your toys. Most of all be inventive with your locations and backdrops and ideas - this is business not just a throw away picture on Grindr and Scruff. It is also good to change your main image etc. about once a month to make your ad look fresh and stop you appearing like unnoticeable wallpaper to potential purchasers. Often it is difficult to represent yourself in just one image so make it a very good one, well thought out as customers will not look at your next 10 pics or so if the lead one (which as mentioned above may have to be a PC one unfortunately) does not entice them and they will move on to another Ad.

DESCRIPTION - The next most important thing is your title. If you are a known model then your name is all you need otherwise just 'Steve' or 'Luke' just won't cut it amongst the large number of other Ads saying the same. You need something exciting probably between 1 and 5 words that peaks a customer's interest to investigate more and look at your longer description further down. I have used many over the years and a good one was 'Military Holewrecker' in two words it hinted at my uniformed army past and also underlined I am a total top, hung and verbal and it made me a lot of money. So did other titles like RawPornStar, HorsehungMarine, BarebackCop and ArmyBreeder all doing the business but I am sure you get the idea. If you are a gymnast, cage fighter, truck driver, security guard etc or and this is just as good....look like one and can pull it off, then lead with it. The idea whatever you do is to make yourself stand out from the other 1000 or so escorts who are being fucking lazy in their marketing and never going to make the big bucks that you will.

Beyond the title you can put as much information in your fuller description as you want but make it interesting, really horny and exciting and possibly amusing just remember though that clients are looking to meet an escort not read a novel.

INFORMATION - Going from the older days of magazine ads often where you are paying monthly per word or letter there are many abbreviations that are well-known. Some are obvious like DP, CP, XXL and BJ whereas others are much more specific to the industry which most clients will know. These are shortened terms like ATM - ass to mouth, PSE -Porn star experience, CIM -Cum In Mouth or BFE -Boyfriend experience. There are over 700 of these in common usage which you can easily find online and maybe start finding which ones you want to push and apply to you and also get used to them as clients will refer to the abbreviated terms in phone calls etc. Obviously, most adverts now will not be in print but the same rules apply to digital escort marketing or indeed limited length texts.

Try and make your customers life as easy as possible by making all the most important facts visible early on. Things like your location, time availability, whether you do incalls or outcalls and how to get in touch should all be front and central and no point holding back on. If you have toys, large sex equipment like fuck machines or milking machines, maybe a sling, fetish gear or whatever then put it out there. Also, if there are things you do not do like say mixed couples as you are not into the opposite sex, unprotected sex, calls after midnight, take withheld number calls or whatever mention it to save hassle, disgruntled customers or issues down the road. Likewise, many escorts are genuinely providing a non-sexual company service possibly for a traveller on their own for the night, dinner, a business trip or holiday companion then make it clear. Muscle worship is also a big industry and non-sexual as is massage - just make it absolutely clear at some point early in your description. Think long and hard about what you write and review it regularly especially when you get any feedback good or bad from customers and fine tune all aspects of this part of your marketing to a high degree. Sometimes edited profiles appear higher up in searches. Maybe put yourself in the position of the client looking at your Ad and see what he sees, thinks and what information is missing or you are holding back and act accordingly. Also, look at other escort Ads and profiles for ideas and suggestions that you think are cool and that you can utilise but don't plagiarize. For example, one of the things that very few escorts mention is whether they kiss or not and this is often a biggie with customers so if you do then list it and increase your bookings.

Your nationality and race maybe a bonus in your market. When in Australia clients tend to want an Australian escort rather than say a Brazilian or Brit and of course vice versa. Many guys really want to hire a black, Asian, Caucasian or Latino escort and there are no poor cards here as they are all selling points so use them accordingly. If you have a big dick then mention it's size as 9x7 will get your phone going provided you are telling the truth or as good as…note dicksizes tend to still be in imperial inches rather than metric centimeters more often than not. Many escorts tell fibs about say being ex-forces, virgins or having sexy/horny jobs and my view is this is fine providing you can deliver and you follow through with it as it can be very successful marketing and takes us back to the above where the whole point is to stand out from all the other boring, bland, middle ground escorts that pollute the industry and always will do. This brings us nicely to the subject of an escorts age. Every age has its admirers and clients but of course there is a tendence to knock a few years off and your real age is rarely the same as your escort/business age and there is nothing wrong with that as it has always gone on, always will do and nothing anyone can do to change it. A 21yo will claim to be 18 (If legal in that territory) and a 55yo will claim to be 45 if you can physically pull it off and do and look the business. I tend to think that many customers factor this in anyway but it is a state of the game that youth is a bigger seller for many. That said of course, daddies are a huge escort market but again the age will always be massaged downwards.

PRICE - We will cover this in greater detail later but for now you just have one decision to make do you list your price per hour, second hour, nightly rate and weekend rate or do you just put something like 'rate on request'. It does not take major research by a client to establish roughly what the going rate is in a specific City so this is not about being clever. The main difference is basically if you list your price then only those that can afford you will contact you which will cut down the timewasters and price shoppers but they may not call at all. On the other side if there is no price listed then they have to contact you for this which will increase the number of inquiries but also massively the number of timewasters or 'not your client' types but the upside is they may like your voice, attitude or some such and you may be able to talk them into a successful hire.....but this will increase your time usage. Personally, I have always listed my rates for an easy life and therefore everyone who calls is already a long way down the road to a physical meet but I have a lot of industry colleagues who prefer the non-disclosure route (you will of course have to name your rate at some point and maybe you are open to negotiation and haggling which was personally never for me).

The last thing to consider is whether you just place your Ad amongst everyone else's and hope for the best more often than not as a free one or do you pay for prominent/first page/higher up visibility. This can prove quite costly but undoubtedly it does work as many clients like searches on Google do not progress too far past the first or second pages. My opinion would be that if you are a full-time escort or have a lot of slots then it is money well spent whereas if you have a full-time job and just escort some occasional nights or at the weekend it may not be worth you paying the premium charges. Remember that a huge number of clients if you are any good will be repeat customers who will already have your number so no advertising or bonus payments are needed for their custom

11 TIMEWASTERS

As a gay fetish journalist for more than 18 years I have interviewed all the great and good of the queer world including the major porn stars many of which were and are some of the most successful escorts of all time. One common denominator without question was that if I ever asked them what was the worst thing about escorting the answer was always timewasters.

They come in so many shapes and sizes and after 25 years I can spot a lot of them but still not all. There are guys who message you from 2000 miles away, those that need to discuss your availability and interests as 'they are coming to your city', guys who want to book you 2 or 3 days in advance or indeed those that contact you for 'right now' seem genuine but are in fact full of BS.....of course none of these will become clients and they know it from the outset. If that is not enough then there is the army of cyber sexers or picture collectors. Often they are just after phone sex and getting you to talk about horny stuff for free under the guise of a potential what will become fantasy booking before cowardly hanging up. You will get them daily and although there are no stats I would estimate that 75% of inquiries will just waste your valuable time and the (never gone be) client knows it the second they pick up the phone or type the first word.

I have had clients walking down my street asking if it is by so and so bar or by the pink house and still they don't show and it will drive you crazy if you take everyone at face value.

It is not done by the same people, have a pattern or done by an organised group so you cannot truthly always spot them. So, what can you do?

As mentioned previously, put as much information including age, location, price and services in your profile or Ad as possible, this will limit some of the needless questions. If they phone from a withheld number then this automatically should get your warning lights flashing but not always but certainly a indicator. If they want to talk or ask what you are into or indeed can you get other tops/bottoms etc. these are all massive signs of the lesser spotted timewaster. If they offer you a high inducement rate then although tempting there is a great chance that you will regret taking that booking or call....even clients with Millions of dollars want value for money and do not offer you sums like a $1000 upfront. Every seasoned escort will develop their own rules the trouble is that there are genuine, nervous, straight or first-timers amongst them so my view is where possible to always engage for a LIMITED period. Stay business like and do not get drawn into sex talk. Personally, if they are not discussing money by the third question on the phone or text then I start to wind it up fast. If you hear heavy breathing or guys not talking in a business-like manner instead using a 'what are you wearing' type sleaze voice or manner then move on asap. Do not get into long discussions about services, use professional words rather than horny verbal and drive them towards a booking rather than an ongoing i have all the time in the World chat....they have spare time but you don't.

There is little point phoning them back, reporting them or texting them later as it achieves nothing and is just a further waste of your time. Likewise, there are no databases or review sites really worth putting them on so you just need to develop broad shoulders in dealing with it as it will happen to you, whoever you are each and every day of your escort career. The truth is that they have sad little lives often relatively sexless with far too much time on their hands and you are being paid big bucks to have great sex with wonderful clients, meet people, travel and experiment so hold your head up and be positive. If you have serious or repeated issues with a client or timewaster then these are the exception and you can then move them onto a report site but not 99% of them who are little more than annoying chancers and tbh they come with the job so except it.

If you are doing incalls then there is less hassle as they are just no shows. You can ask them in this modern technology age to message before they leave and on route and if they don't or make some excuse like their phone is broken, low on batteries etc then i will 100% guarantee you they have no intention of meeting and never did You can always exchange live map location on your smart phone that maybe help you sort the wannabe's from the genuine clients and stop you endlessly running around your house putting on rugby kit for something which will never be and the client is just not being straight with you. For outcalls you can get them to pay for your Uber or if in a hotel you can phone the front desk and check the room number and name before you set off. To be honest though if someone just gives you a false address to get you talking or so that they can watch from across the street there is little you can do to stop this from happening and you have to just put it down as a bad day at the office and one of the unstoppable negatives of what is really one of the best jobs in the World. If they want you to drive any distance (say 20kms), or book an overnight, weekend etc then ask for a 50% deposit upfront - if they have issues with this then move on as he was never your serious client. Obviously with trains or overseas flights it is the industry standard that the client buys the ticket in advance and issues them to you which is all the proof you need that they are genuinely looking for business. I have never tried it but with readily available online banking and services such as PayPal you could ask for a deposit every time to secure the booking but as this is far from industry standard many good customers may get offended by this and move on loosing you a chunk of your business and with each client possibly paying you your weekly rent that could be a substantial loss to you. Remember if getting a client to book a travel ticket for you to give him your legal name rather than your porn or model name which will match up with your photo ID and save expensive ticket name changes.

If you let them and don't have any rules or are desperate for clients/work/money they will drive you crazy and although over time you will spot them sooner you will never spot them all and they will indeed keep coming like a plague of masturbating self-abusing zombies.

12 GAY FOR PAY, FAKING IT OR 'TRADE' AS IT IS OFTEN KNOWN

Escorting is a fantastic way to make money, a career or a living. As established if you have something others will pay for then you are in business. The trouble is what happens if you are not attracted to an audience that wants to hire you. In the straight world it is pretty route one and guys will hire girls & have done for millennia the problem is that in the moralistic world females who sleep around a lot or charge for sex are deemed unfairly as sluts, slags, cheap, not the marrying kind, second class citizens, failures, desperate or whatever. This is extremely harsh and an old-fashioned view but all i can do is reflect on how society perceives female escorts historically. The ones i know are great, very professional, expert business women and in charge of what they do and where they are going and can handle any flack that comes their way. So provided they can handle any social brickbats and finger pointing then they are good to go.

A straight guy wishing to sell his services has a different social issue to deal with. They may have little stigma from society for what they do and in fact they might have

THE ULTIMATE GUIDE TO BECOMING A SUCCESSFUL ESCORT

bragging rights with other males but this historically is a pretty bad business model. Simply less women are prepared to pay for sex largely for the above reputation reasons and of course if they want a shag there are millions of horny men out there wanting to get another notch on their bedpost and will do the deed for no money. Basically, the straight male being hired for sex or company by females is a very small market indeed. Simply, your phone will not go often if at all however fit and hung you are, it is just the state of play even nowadays in the 2020's.

In straight porn there is the same issue. Women get the big money, appear on the film covers, adverts and posters and become stars whilst the men are largely just an unfortunate prop required. Very few men can make a decent living as a male porn star in the straight world and often they will be paid as little as 100 bucks a day.......usually the female star will make 5/10 or 15 times the money of her male co-star. This is because almost any man will fuck a female porn star for free if given half the chance and as he is not what the viewer is coming to the film to watch why pay him decent money.....basic supply and demand.

So, we have the case where women in the adult and sex industry will probably suffer some social stigma but if they can deal with it or keep it secret they will hopefully have great and long lasting careers in a very big lucrative market. Straight men can work without any stigma hopefully but they are likely to be pretty poor earners.

In the male gay world their escorts and porn stars are the kings of the world with no stigma and in fact are pursued, well paid and put on a pedestal. The stigma they may suffer unfortunately may come from their sexuality alone which thankfully is becoming less of an issue but it is still there. Which brings us to the term 'Gay For Pay' that started in the adult film industry but now the term equally applies to escorting.

A straight guy 'pretending' to be gay will get many times the hourly/daily rate for being with another man on film and if he escorts he will be a thousand times busier being hired by guys than by women. This could require a large mental leap and he may struggle but if he can handle it, pull off a suitable act and indeed be able to perform then he will likely have a much bigger and better career. There are many well-known gay porn stars who have wives and kids. They tend to also operate in the straight markets too which i guess is more enjoyable or natural to them but they need the pink dollar to pay their bills.

When you see a guys advert it will not declare he is 'gay for pay' as this will not help him in any way so clients need to be aware of this (He may sometimes declare himself as bisexual of course). Invariably GtoP guys tend to get a bad rap from fellow escorts and performers (they often get loads of bad reviews too). It is well known in the gay porn industry as a golden rule that you never cast two GtoP guys in the same scene which will invariably end up not working. So, if you are straight and want to escort you will almost certainly have to have some levels of gay sex so best get your head around that at the outset. Bi-guys and indeed women have a more straightforward situation but the end result is the same & that is in the high 90 percentage range where it is guys that hire escorts and always has been. Maybe nowadays with many successful business women in good rolls this might start to change but the social stigma referred to earlier will take a long while to alter regardless.

FALSE NAMES

Almost all escorts use false names and often several of them. Firstly, their own name maybe pretty boring and unexciting so like pop stars and movie stars a more interesting or memorable one is used. More readily fake names are used for security, privacy and secrecy. Any name can be picked and in the escort world little more than a horny first name is all you need. Unless you are famous for something else like say Big Brother reality TV star Steven Daigle or real life military man Marc McAulay then i would always advise getting a pseudonym if for no other reason than it stops your granny accidentally seeing pictures of your cock or indeed your old school mates or teachers accidentally coming across your advert. There is a technical bonus nowadays in that you can choose a name that shows up better in search engines than on social media whereas Jack Smith maybe the escort name you want but nobody will ever find you online as you will be lost with millions of other civilians with the same name. To be honest if i knew back then what i know now i would not have picked the name Paul Stag which is a great masculine name i associated with a proud rampant strong Scottish deer but twenty five years on it is lost on Google amongst a load of posts and pictures of guys called Paul who are having a stag do (bachelor party).

There are long term benefits of having a separate adult and escort identity too. If you through a work or personal issue decide to move on in your life you can merely kill off your alter ego and delete him online. Of course your images will be out there for eternity but it is a very good start if and when you need a clean break. Also far be it for me to advocate anything illegal but a pseudonym can help with your tax situation too as earnings under your created name many of which will be in cash and without formal receipts for obvious reasons will give you scope in that area....that said i have always annually declared my tax earnings from escorting and the adult industry partly because they were too obvious and because it gave me a lot of headroom to claim back as valid expenses everything from sex toys, to poppers, clothing and a multitude of equipment used in escorting my fruitier customers.

NON-SEXUAL SERVICES

Legally as mentioned earlier escorts are selling their time rather than any specific sex acts but it would be naive to think that this is not going to come up during the majority of standard hires. Yet there are many exceptions that straight guys, bi-guys or those with partners who have concerns can consider.

Guys may hire you genuinely for your company or a date - maybe a boyfriend experience or to accompany them to an important personal or business event and this type of hire may not require sex. The biggest and most well-known area is massage where a client may want a perfectly valid body rub with no 'happy-ending'.

Lots of guys provide 'naked' services such as acting as a butler, waiter at a party, decorator, hairdresser, cleaner in the nude. The client may want a fantasy which does not revolve around sex....Two that i get a lot is that guys hire me to put them through verbal military exercises or to beat them up (safely) a little bit.....but largely or indeed completely non sexual.

Many so called sex acts like the use of toys, masturbation, circle jerking, corporal punishment, foot worship etc. can always be done by escorts making good money without being true gay sex acts shall we say. Then there is the lucrative world of body worship where guys will pay usually very muscular guys to do no more than pose for them in shorts or swimming trunks with maybe a bit of touching but nothing close to sex and loads of straight guys do this very successfully. There is often an added bonus for the muscular market in that clients or fans may finance your muscle development and pay for your expensive protein shakes, vitamins and supplements. Furthermore, there is the area of 'Findom' or cash masters where customers will pay you to abuse them verbally or electronically and make them feel like 'slaves' or 'subs' without it ever leading too ever getting close to the area of a meet or sexual activity. In conclusion, if for some reason you do not wish to have sex as part of your service then there are a number of lucrative avenues to investigate - provided as i keep saying you have something of interest that someone will pay for. Make it clear, keep it real and stay focused on that and don't get talked into doing something you do not want too or have not agreed to do. Remain professional at all times.

It is worth underlying the 'company' aspect of escorting as this is often overlooked. If you are a good conservationist, witty, charming, intelligent and well presented then this area can be even more lucrative than a straight forward one hour shag or a guy who has a big knob. It is wonderful and an honour for a client to pay you a substantial sum to merely enjoy a nice meal, visit a club or party or accompany him to a gay bar or sauna where they are nervous or unsure. The important thing is to agree a lump rate or hourly rate at the outset and this should include every minute you are together whether eating, drinking, dancing or watching a show; your time is valuable and you should be compensated in full. Of course the client should also pay for any venue entrance fees, drinks or ancillaries in full for both of you and this brings us to the whole point of the oldest industry in World which is the subject of money.

13 MONEY & RATES

So, you have always wanted to try your hand at escorting and earn $100,000 per year just by fucking Professional footballers up the ass? You think you are a great fuck, decent looking and could really do with all that extra cash you have heard they make but how lucrative is it and what should you charge?. Well, the going basic rate is about at $200-250/hour for an incall at your place or plus travel for outcalls which is truly great money and in fact similar to professional lawyer/ accountant rates to be honest although the work is a lot more fun. The rate can be lower if you wish or much higher depending on a number of factors some of which we will drill into below. You could make a years national average salary (30,000 Euros) in just 2 weeks with just your ass but if it was that easy why isn't everyone doing it well the simple reason is that they can but most don't do it well which is why the average lifespan of a new escort's career is just 12 weeks.

Money is what makes the industry go round, the soul reason it exists and starting at the rates above it will soon build up for you and will continue for as long as you want if you follow the guidance and tips in this book. The big names which are usually the ones that have been in studio porn or have some degree of celebrity or notoriety in the industry or the most professional with serious repeat clients make an awful lot more as clients often book for multiple hours, overnights, weekends or longer holiday/business trips. You are unique and can cultivate your own fanbase and then if a guy wants to hire you he will pay above the standard as he wants you and only you.....this is the goal to aim for but let's do the basics first before the top of the tree'

You have your hourly rate which you think is fair and achievable.....if you need any guidance do a bit of research and see what others are charging but do not under value yourself or more importantly your time. When you get inquiries, i don't but you can negotiate your rates somewhat depending how busy you are etc. must real clients tend to know the rough going rate anyway in a region before first contact. Nowadays unlike 20 years ago you will often know what the client looks like which is helpful and although i am not proud of it if i do not fancy the guy i have been known to charge a little more for guys or services on the edge of my personal taste. There is a lot of industry opinion as to whether you advertise your rate or just put something like 'price on application'. The latter opens the door for negotiation both up and down which you might like or be uncomfortable with but personally i prefer to lead everywhere with my flat rate to stop the endless timewasters who can and will continually contact you valuing your time at a paltry 30 bucks an hour or some such. If they see an advert for you at say $200/hour then that should stop many cheap inquiries and anyone who does call in theory (but not practice) has the cash for your time and the booking turning into reality will depend on whether you have the service etc he wants or as it is known 'you are the right escort for that client'... the other factor will of course be how serious the client is in an actual hire or is he just a fanatasist looking for a quick bit of phone sex at your cost.....or hoping to catch you on the cheap when you are feeling horny (never go down this last route as prices can never be increased in future).

There is a rough industry rule of thumb that subsequent hours after the first one are slightly discounted say by 20 or 30 Euros/Dollars per hour with overnights (Fix the time in advance) 11-7AM at about 800 - 1200 or weekends being 2,000 - 2,500. The length of the booking which will probably have and require other topic discussions will always be a negotiation, just do not get too carried away as the basic rate is better than what most guys in other jobs are earning ie do not get greedy. Ninety eight percent of escorts are self-employed with very few using an agency so you can sort your own fees accordingly but whichever way you cut it this is great money and if you get it right the sky is the limit. Porn star Junior Stellano made $20,000 for one holiday with a client and they may have only had sex a handful of times whereas bareback superstar Chad Brock was given a car by one of his repeat clients so the dream at the top of that tree is there to be grasped.

There are a lot of bad and dodgy escorts out there and please do not be one of them. Repeat clients, a good name and good reviews are the goal and way more valuable than a quick buck upfront for some dodgy service or practice......a bad reputation will always come back to haunt you. You are being paid fantastic money that others can only dream off often for just having fun so be respectful, prompt, interesting and treat your clients well and they will return for sure once they have tried your chancer escort competitors. Many of my regulars have said they tried other before or for variety but most are not great value and they prefer to return and these guys become friends effectively and many have been with me for years which makes the best job in the World even more pleasant and basically easier.

Cash has always been king in the adult industry but like everywhere else times are changing as we become an increasingly cashless society. You can ask and get cash and many clients prefer this as it effectively leaves no paper trail back to husbands, wives or whatever. Many, as these are often quite large sums will want to do bank transfers which often means you get paid upfront so get a bank account also Paypal or similar are very easy and nowadays there are easy hand held credit card machines for you to get the money directly (do not expect all banks to give you handheld devices as they sometimes have moral issues with the adult industry even if entirely legal in that territory. Act like a business be set up with as many methods as you can as this will come across as professional rather than expecting guys to have $1500 in cash tucked away in their bedside cabinets.

If you have any doubts about a client as regards your security then my view would be to not do that job at all but you can always ask for a 50% deposit upfront which might ease any considerations that the customer is a timewaster or will start renegotiating when you arrive or finish. A deposit should always be obtained if travelling any major distance to a client and he to be honest should expect that.

Whether you collect the money at the start of the hour or at the end is up to you. It is classier and more standard to get it at the end and it is sexier if it is hardly referred too; hence seeing your money by the bed and just politely collecting it at the end with little fanfare will make the customer feel less used or desperate possibly.....a feeling you are always trying to avoid. Always check the amount quickly. I have always taken money at the end and it has very rarely been a problem the exceptions are when you get a vibe that the guy is high or judging by his accommodation may not have a lot of spare cash and then occasionally I do ask to settle up after a couple of minutes into the booking, but always be prepared to walk away. No one client or pay day is worth the hassle or long-term issues a bad client will do. I know lots of escorts who collect the money on arrival and clients that offer it and really it is just your call of course the digitizing of many transactions have often taken the payment a long way away from the actual meeting and its energy which i have found to be helpful and a positive step. One note though is i am ex-military and an ex-cop and a pretty big muscular guy so can handle a situation if someone is getting silly or has bad intentions as regards payment, so possibly i have been given an easier ride in the industry by default. If you are a young twinky guy or similar you may want to alter your service more and get the money upfront so as you can relax and know that you are not going to be ripped off. As regards general security we will come to that later.

According to the tax authorities there are only a couple of thousand escorts in the World and this includes women, this means that the majority of escorts are doing it as extra cash on the side or as part of the black market which obviously we cannot condone but this industry is incredibly hard to Police. If you do declare it as taxable income you will open up a Pandora's box of expenses you can claim from toys to travel from trainers/clothes to vehicle repairs anything you can say you use for sex from cucumbers to baseball bats as well as general household service bills such as heating/water but only do this obviously if escorting is legal in your country. My tax office knows fully about me being an escort and luckily i am in the UK where it is all legal and they once said to me if i was randomly ever investigated one year it is more than likely that the tax guy or team would be more fascinated about the industry compared to all their normal cases that it would be a walk in the park.

14 ESCORT TALES - BRIAN BONDS

I've had a lot of stories throughout my eleven years in sex work. One of my favorite memories was being invited back to a hotel with a bunch of the performers at Hustlaball in Las Vegas to a client's room who wanted to sit back and watch all of us play together. It's one thing to get booked with another escort, who may just so happen to be a friend or boyfriend, but to get hired with a bunch of them just to fuck each other was such a huge turn on for me. We had all just performed until 3am, and we just kept wanting each other. More readily there wasn't a chance to play with somebody you fancied at Hustlaball as everyone was working but then you get to do what you like at the impromptu private party. Plus, there is the extra bonus of getting paid. Getting paid to sexually perform with your friends, who are among the sexiest in the world, for the enjoyment of another is, and will forever be, the greatest job I've ever had.

15 EQUIPMENT NEEDED

In effect the only thing you really need is a decent mobile phone as mentioned earlier with clear barriers from all the other elements of your personal telephone/smartphone life.

You should also have with you at all times and provide for the client the Four must haves of all escorts.

1   Lubrication - do not expect the client to have it especially if he is on a business trip or straight.
2   Condoms - Your sexual health is all important. If you catch sexually transmitted diseases, you will be out of business for a week or so. Bareback/Condomless/Freedom of choice is predominant in the escort world but that said you may wish to protect yourself from HIV, Hep C or regular STI's or your client may wish too. Most escorts nowadays offer both covered and uncovered sex but regardless you should always have some rubbers with you.
3   Poppers - The client may have them but you should always have some relatively fresh ones (stored in your refrigerator) to hand. Many of your clients will be inexperienced or anal virgins and offering these may make the difference between a successful or poor session. Use sparingly.

4   Viagra or similar - Just in case you or the client
    struggle to get wood they are cheap and cheerful
    nowadays and often useful. Regularly these days you
    will know what the client looks like beforehand but
    sometimes you will not and if you really don't fancy
    him or her then it is best to have all the artificial help
    you can get easily. Personally, i have never injected
    my cock with Trimix/Caverject or similar with a
    client only using those for film or stage appearances.
    They are a bit pricey at say 20 bucks a go and of
    course repeated use often will not be good for your
    cock and future natural boners not to mention your
    mental dependence on them that will creep into your
    mind. In my view if you have to inject to have a
    client then you may not have a high enough sex drive
    for this job and escorting is not for you. Remember
    that some bookings will be timewasters and pre-
    injecting will be bad news financially and health wise
    for a no-show and injecting whilst with the client
    may be somewhat awkward and is borderline rude.

We will cover drugs and chems later but do not drift
into a business of supplying substances to punters as
down this road this is where the biggest problems lie.
If they are not interested in sex but just want you to
supply stuff then you are not an escort but a drug dealer
and that will i guarantee you end up disastrously. Many
clients will want you to be in the same chem headspace
as them but this always leads to bad business practice
especially as regards your valuable time, over extended
unrewarded sessions and will undoubtedly cause you
'habit' problems very quickly. Personally, as an escort or
otherwise i have never done any chems in my life which

i believe is one of the biggest reasons i am still here and have been able to always be professional.

Personally, as the best clients are often of the 'right now' variety i always have a rucksack packed with the main 4 above and many other items covering most mainstream sex acts ready to go. This stops last minute rushing around and off course forgetting something basic or specifically asked for especially with a last-minute late at night booking.

Besides the lube, poppers, condoms and Viagra my outcall bag (which is just as valuable for incalls really having everything in one place) contains the following:-

Business cards
Cock Rings
Autograph photos and sharpie (Many clients are fans)
A small and larger dildo
Vibrator
Cigars
Small electro set
Cumrag
Rank Jockstrap
Butt plug
Clothe pegs
Metal nipple clamps
Cat-o-nine tails whip
Paddle
Toothbrush
A Porn DVD
Dental gag
Fisting lube

Disposable gloves
Hairnet for asphyxiation play
Shoelaces
Hand cuffs
Rubber chain of balls
Candle and lighter for hot wax
Cotton wool buds for sounding
Speculum
Ball weight
Parachute
Nail File
Blindfold.

.....yes, they all do fit in one rucksack and no you do not have to use them all every time or indeed any of them they are simply always to hand at home or on an outcall if you or the client wants to get inventive, experiment and make it more memorable.....or indeed failed to discuss some interest in the pre-booking call discussion.

I am a top and have provided besides company, role play and vanilla service also a relatively fetish service. This may not be you and therefore many of the above will not apply and you may not know what they are or indeed used for which is fine but the point remains whatever you are offering have it all together in one place all the time especially as I said for 'right now' customers who may be your majority or late night last minute bookings

I in the same vein as above offer a number of looks. Obviously with my slightly public past & in line with my targeted advertising have military, police, leather and rugby as a given. I also have soccer kit, wrestling, boxer, smart suits, skinhead, rubber, builder/tradie gear, a kilt etc, etc. This may not apply to you but selling fantasies is a good area and the investment can be done over time. Ok so it's a bit Village People but it means that my repeat clients don't get bored and it separates you from your competitors, it's fun, my customers like it and you could charge extra for it (I personally do not). Part of our business is or can be selling a fantasy.

Similarly, some escorts may be specialising in certain sex acts like say fisting, corporal punishment, foot worship, bondage, BDSM or whatever and likewise this separates you from the throng, can often be charged at a premium and channels you presumably directly into an area you actually enjoy. Clients in this area will want to know what equipment you have whether it be fuck machines, a wet room, sling, milking machines, types of canes, restraint facilities or even a 'dungeon' 'bespoke play-space' so market it accordingly which can save you a lot of phone or text time. If specialising, ensure your customers know about it. This does require investment but these areas are very lucrative and being harder to find by punters led to a much higher rate of repeat business. Simply you have a lot less competitors.

In conclusion, once you have worked out what service you are going to supply get the kit you need. Keep it clean and in good maintenance and in one place. You should aim to be more than a chancer escort after a quick buck now and then instead you should be a true professional providing a quality well thought out and equipped service....You are an elite escort, a professional treating it as a career rather than a quick money grab.

16 FIRST CONTACT

So, you have launched your business, made you plan and worked out your marketing and fully taken on board that time is money i.e. your time is worth a lot of money. Now customers should start approaching you on a regular basis. You will need a mobile phone ideally for your own sanity with a different number to the ones that your friends, family and business colleagues use. It is always good to know that every call coming in is from a potential or existing client possibly looking for sex rather than from your mother or bank manager so as you are in the right head space for a horny business call (This also makes sense for text and WhatsApps that you may not wish to open in public etc also it can keep stalkers and problem guys at arms length somewhat.

Many clients will have a similar idea for security and use withheld numbers to contact you which is fair enough and some escorts won't take calls from these numbers and advertise as such. This is your call as there are some great discrete and sometime famous guys who use withheld numbers but equally it is hugely adopted by time wasters after cyber sex chat or guys who will organise false meetings. Personally, I have always answered them but i am instantly on my guard and if the wrong questions come up then i am quickly on my way to the next client. If a client is not talking normally like in a weird voice they are probably jerking off and are not your clients, likewise if they start asking what you are into or start talking dirty then you are onto a loser. My personal rules are that if we are not discussing rates by the third question then i bring it up and if it gets to Seven questions then i am almost certainly going to curtail the call. If they ask for your overnight rate or weekend rate then this if you have never met the guy before is also relatively often but not always going to be a waste of time and not lead to a booking. Keep it on business and don't get sidetracked and as in many aspects of live if it sounds too good to be true then it always will be and they are not wealthy businessmen or want a holiday companion to the Caribbean all expenses paid....instead they just want to keep you talking as they bust a nut there end for free. One of the most important questions that is overlooked by both parties is do you kiss and for many clients this is important but they rarely remember to ask it so you can volunteer it which will more often be a plus and help towards closing a deal.

Most escorts will use a false name or several and if you have a bespoke telephone then you will expect your pseudonym to be used which will lead to less confusion. I would never advise any escort or adult performer to use their family name unless there is a genuine positive reason to do so.

I advise clients to ask whatever questions that they are interested in but to be concise and this applies to escorts also. Where are you and when are you looking for are the sort of things you can get too right at the start. Your job is to weed the genuine clients out from the wannabes and time wasters at every step. If they are phoning weeks in advance for a future visit to your area then it will never result in a meet. If they are phoning a day or so in advance then again this is quite a warning sign and almost certainly all talk with no action; and certainly don't change any future personal plans for an 'advance' booking from a client of 12 hours plus in my view. You can also ask a client to message when he is leaving and on his way which may help you spot someone who is genuine more readily. If doing an outcall (especially to a withheld number) then try and satisfy yourself with questions that this is going to be an actual meet - clients may give you false addresses that do not exist or are not their own places. Over time you will spot most of these but you will probably never catch them all before it is too late. Obviously with hotel bookings you can phone the front desk beforehand with a story to check the client is in that room.

With smart phone messages never delete them as this can indicator months or years later who are your repeat timewasters and in fact on my phone i am now up to 'Timewaster 1,545' down under my contacts.

Nowadays with the phone and internet you can have a lot more security and weapons to spot genuine guys from timewasters but the latter unfortunately will never stop coming so develop your own systems to protect your time and business. Uber type taxi services are a great new addition in that you can ask the client to send you one over and as he is paying for your travel if genuine he should be fine with this and it is almost like a mini type deposit which does indeed bring us to outcalls.

OUTCALLS

This is where the client wants you to visit him as opposed to him coming to you as an Incall if you are in a position to accommodate clients. You must always charge for you expected travel costs and the time you will be travelling and as mentioned previously if any sort of distance get 50% deposit transferred beforehand. In my experience you will get just about as many outcalls as incalls so hopefully for a successful business you will put yourself in a position to provide both services.

If a client wants a lot of paraphernalia like an outfit, sex toys or equipment then maybe encourage him to come to you as although you can carry a certain amount of kit it is impractical for him to ask you to bring three bags of stuff on the bus to his. That said once a client is a repeat customer then you can start changing up some of your rules as you know he is genuine and is a valid paying customer. Also to keep him as a client for longer similar to partnered sex if you introduce variety he is likely to stay with you for many more months and years possibly.

There no set rate to charge on top of your hourly rate for an outcall but even if he is walking distance charge something like 20 bucks minimum for your time. If when you meet the session does not happen because one side or other has a change of heart then he should still give you something like 40 bucks for your trouble.

If a client wants you out of town or overseas then it is industry standard to get him to send you your ticket paid for in advance. If flying then remember to ensure he books the ticket in your given family name as in your passport rather than your escort name.

DO NOT TRAVEL ANY DECENT DISTANCE WITHOUT A DEPOSIT....EVER!

17 THE SESSION

You will probably be nervous at first but then so will the client. It is only sex, be professional and have fun. If in a hotel check with the front desk before heading out to ensure the client is in that room number. Maybe phone him from the foyer so he is ready for you or message on your mobile when just a few minutes away. Maybe pop a quarter of a Viagra beforehand so you don't have to worry about getting hard.

Have a little chat at the start as this will relax both of you and eat into the time but remember you are on the clock and this is work and he is almost more interested in other things than your personality. At the start you could ask for the money but it is more regular and classier in my view to get paid at the end. Despite urban myths it is largely unheard of for a client not to pay so concentrate on giving him a good time. Take the lead in getting the ball rolling. Put all your personal items and clothes in one place as leaving things at a clients maybe impossible to retrieve and at the very least it is a headache for you.

Take some toys with you as well as rubbers, lube and poppers, these are now tools of your trade. Don't clock watch but be aware of the time and after an hour and a quarter say bring the session to a close and politely ask for the money and suggest he keeps your number for next time. You can take breaks or even suggest this to him as he is probably expecting a realistic session rather than employing a machine or robot for 60 minutes. If you have trouble closing the job then fake an orgasm which brings it to a natural close. Some clients will give you a tip if they have had fun and of course the golden goose is to get repeat clients who book you once a week or every time they are in town which is in effect guaranteed money with a guy you know and trust for no advertising cost.

Try and introduce the client to new things, suggest rimming, spanking, fisting, electro, watersports, roleplay etc they will thank you for it and always come back to you. Variety also breaks the session up for you as the client has chosen you rather than the other way around and you need to keep engaged. Similarly, it is a good way to keep your interest in sex long term rather than it becoming like a conveyor belt to you which believe me will show over time in your face, engagement, body language and attitude.

If an incall at your place put all your valuables out of temptations way, get a glass of water ready for the client and some porn on the TV or computer. If you are asked to travel any sort of distance then agree the fee fully, get 50% deposit upfront via bank transfer or Paypal before setting out. If he does not agree to this then move onto the next client as he is going to be problematic. The golden rule is always listen to your gut and act on it from initial first conversation through to a physical meet. The famous 'Escort Trap is where many guys offer you the world but are just having a fantasy wank and give false addresses etc and then you are out of pocket. If you get an overseas booking then the client pays for the hotel, flight, all expenses as well as your fee in advance and don't begin to take it seriously and cancel things or take days off work until the flight tickets have turned up.

If you feel uncomfortable for any reason then leave or if an incall bring the session to a close. No one individual fee is worth the hassle you may get and the psychology and thought processes that you will linger much longer with you than a couple of hundred dollars. It may turn you off the job altogether which would be a shame. You will get great clients and you will get bad ones and i am not talking about looks or physicality. How you handle them, maybe learn from them or whatever will be a huge factor in whether you are in the job for just a few weeks or a very long lucrative career whether full or part-time.

18 REVIEWS

This is a new phenomenon due to the World Wide Web that can only make things better for the industry and harder for the many poor escorts with shoddy services that our clients have had to suffer for years. In the past if a client had a bad experience all he could do is suck it up and maybe give a little bad word of mouth to his mates. Nowadays, many of the better escorts work hard to ensure their clients have a good time and the best thank you is to take the time and write a little review online....many customers actually enjoy writing the reviews especially if you are a bit of a porn star etc.

The trouble is that as we do not have one world renowned escort site like 10 years ago with Rentboy. com (RIP) no review becomes universally good, useful or bad. So, there is a multitude of regional escort sites and platforms some of which have review sections and some that do not. Sites like Sleepyboy have them and both the escorts and clients will find them useful but many great escorts will have no entries so it is not fool proof by any means. Rentmen also has many reviews and they are often similar with just a couple of comments like 'Time spent' 'Are pictures accurate' & 'Would you rehire' which is a great start. Other times you get very detailed paragraphs of the hire which can be useful but off course no two escorts or indeed clients' needs are the same. Unlike say with Trip Advisor or Air BnB here you are basically just looking for the good guys rather than the chancers, money grabbers or bad part-timers. Therefore, to be honest you need little more than a simple indication that the guy will turn up and look and do what he says he will and not rip you off as simple as that. Of course, like in any business not all reviews are legit so the customer should take them as an indicator or extra information rather than gospel. My view is that most clients even happy ones won't write reviews so any unless consistently negative are a very good sign and indicator but should not eclipse a client's own inquiries. If you get a handful of positive reviews you are flying high as you do not need loads as they just won't get read.

You should mention to your client at the end that they may like to leave a review as a nice thank you which is a good policy but off course so many will just not remember to do it or get around to it but the handful that do will stay there forever (and are often not dated anyway). It is always a good policy to find out where the client found you or heard of you anyway so asking politely for a review is just an extension of good business practice. Reviews will get you more bookings and allow you to raise your hourly rate so very definitely worth focusing on but without going over the top as they will never top word of mouth which has and always will be the best 'reviews' ever and what makes the whole industry go around. I have had clients from professional rugby & soccer clubs often guys i recognise from TV and out of the blue you get a second team mate and so on - my record is 5 from one team as obviously reliable and in that case 'discrete' escorts are worth their weight in gold and phone numbers are being passed around in changing rooms quietly between buddies who occasionally like a bit of dick. You cannot beat free advertising ever. Discretion is a huge thing to offer in the escort world and is greatly sort after by often the biggest hirers or the wealthiest/straightest and most successful of clients who are the most likely to rebook (and indeed rebook the same escort rather than constantly be looking for something new each time and risk getting an indiscrete escort or one that attempts some mild form of blackmail).

There are no worthwhile independent review sites away from the main escort hire platforms.....yet

Reviews do work both ways in that there are a number of platforms/websites which enable you to list bad clients under labels like 'Ugly mugs', 'Problem clients' etc. Again, there is no all-encompassing seen by everyone page or database unfortunately. Clients who don't turn up, waste your time, steal or are dangerous can be posted to warn other escorts...these posts are always too late to help you but are useful for the industry and the only decent weapon we have against problem punters....and you will get them. They do become invaluable if you check them in your locale to avoid the simple traps used by clients and to be honest these bad customers will and do repeat and use the same modus operandi each time. This drives you crazy so having some warning kindly posted by others is a big help.

At the end of the day like buying a music CD hiring an escort is one of those few things you are buying relatively on little information.

19 ESCORT TALES - VIKTOR ROM

I was in the city of Shanghai, China 4 years ago and a follower called me asking me to fulfil a sexual fantasy. So, he went looking for his driver and took me to the outskirts of Shanghai and the follower was dressed in a tight shirt, had a muscular body and was wearing women's heels. So, I started the car and began driving and the follower started running in high heels screaming my name after 15 minutes I parked the car and took the follower to an abandoned building where I spread his legs and began to fuck him and then fist him and lift him up while I put my hand in his ass. I was holding him in the air entirely by my fist inside him like a puppet with his high-heels dangling down.

20 DUO'S THREESOMES & GROUPS

Many clients will want a bit more excitement in a session so will be seeking duo's or be in a relationship and want a third for a limited time.

Let's start with Duo's. Maybe you have a partner who will also escort in which case you as a unit will get double money. Alternatively, you may become good friends with another escort or two that you enjoy working with and this is obviously beneficial to all sides as the client gets reliable guys who have some chemistry and each of you can benefit from extra work supplied to you via your mates overflow of business. If you both travel then it is double the travel rate but if one is hosting then obviously only one gets a travel fee.

Often clients will ask you to arrange a second escort which is all very well for them but can create a fortune of work for you. My rule is that if he is not an existing client then he will have to pay a deposit or even better suggest he finds the second guy as hopefully you are happy to work with any other fit professional. Otherwise, the client will have you searching all over town sending pictures on and back for his approval which will take much longer than the actual session.....which maybe a timewaster anyway. Most importantly do not book another escort for an unknown client as if the customer is not genuine, changes his mind or ghost's you then you have an issue on your hands. The upside with your best clients asking for duo's is that you get to pick a guy from your favourite escort website that you fancy and want to play with....whilst someone else is paying you both.

I have done a million duo jobs over time some initiated by me on behalf of a client and some offered to me by other working escorts. The best upside is that you will have another very fit guy there which will help you and undeniably the work load is halved yet the price remains the same.

Three ways in the escort world is where two play mates, partners or even men and women want a third guy in the mix. There is one golden rule with threesomes whether in escorting or not and that is they are very hard to pull off as invariably two tend to connect better and one often feels like a spare wheel. Work hard to avoid this but it is not easy to be honest. It is sometimes but not always the case that an escort increases his rate for two people as opposed to a standard one on one meet. Maybe add $50 or so but don't take the piss. Straight couples often want another guy in the mix and there is obviously two dynamics going on. Firstly, the guy wants to see his wife get fucked by a big dick or some such or equally the guy maybe pretty closeted and it is his way of getting near another naked fit bloke (Maybe in his head without feeling he is gay). If you are going to have trouble getting it up for a woman or if a woman is even in the mix then avoid this work like the plague otherwise go for it and have fun. Your rate should probably stay the same as normal unless you want to add a third person premium. the vibe and dynamic maybe very strange so keep on your toes and have your wits about you as to what the couple actually want from the session as this may not be obvious. Also bear in mind that one half of the couple may be a lot more into the situation than the other so it is a bit of a minefield. Yet, if bisexual or able to pull off this is a nice little lucrative area of additional business coming your way. Personally, i have done married straight couples loads of times and have found them quite easy to do but usually they have been driven by the guys. The men after meeting you may sneakily book one on one gay sessions afterwards and can become good long-lasting clients. There is some market i am not up on where women escorts get employed to join a married straight couple and from what i have been told from my female escort friends this is always the idea of the guy and usually he will want the escort again privately as this is his way of getting around cheating in his head.

It will not stop at three ways though as bigger groups will come into play. This usually comes in the form of sex parties where they want fit guys, younger/older or whatever to be there that will be up for it. These are the best fun and wonderful earners as you are on an hourly rate, plus travel, tips and extras also they are likely to go on longer and have less actual physical work involved. Also, they are a great way of meeting future individual clients. You may be expected to serve drinks or food, maybe put on a strip or a bit of a show and it is all good. You also are unlikely to be the only escort there. These parties may not even be very sexual but who cares if you are being well paid anyway. They are also almost certainly always thrown by relatively wealthy guys where money is no object and their friends are likely to be the same caliber so in effect the best shop window and advertising you can have and hopefully you will still be earning from the original night in various ways for many years to come. Another likely scenario especially on weekends is where guys have druggy parties or get togethers and when guys are high and sexually in the mood there are no guys around who can get hard due to chems so an escort becomes a necessity. Invariably at these events you will not be under huge pressure with a great work load as chemed up guys are very easy to satisfy; just make a point to leave at the agreed time and never agree to be paid in chems...this is your business, career and livelihood not spring break or a Friday night laugh. Also, with groups you may pretty often be paid in advance which is another bonus. Middle Eastern guys when travelling to Europe tend to be very into groups and those well monied will pay for all sorts of whacky sessions - sometimes i have seen 10 escorts in a room with one client just watching paying for the lot but be aware often they are into underage sex and watching an escort or group of escorts have sex with a lad so always be prepared to walk away instantly when the real reason for the session is revealed. That aside i have had many Middle Eastern clients who are always sexually inexperienced and the best i had was when i was paid a large sum in advance (after a prior private meeting) to find 5 other guys all in smart suits to turn up at a Park Lane London hotel and have sex with a guy who was exhausted and ejaculated after just 20 minutes, he then went in the next room whilst we carried on having fun and were all well cashed up.

21 SECURITY

A lot of this comes from common sense but you need to keep your wits about you as you are putting yourself in a vulnerable position relatively often. Security comes in many forms and works both ways with security for the escort and security for the client.

Dodgy clients can be very good at hiding their intent which is more often than not just to waste your time for their own amusement maybe getting you to travel some distance and then ghosting you, never actually having the money or it may be more serious. Firstly, never ever take a meeting without at least one live phone chat, texting or similar only is just not enough. During this you may get a gut feeling of whether this client is good or trouble - in my opinion and experience if your orange warning light is flashing in your head then cancel the appointment and do not re-engage. Nowadays with smart phones and online you will have a phone number trace or a message history with guys maybe going back years to see if you have ever felt uncomfortable or they failed to show up etc. There is a caveat in that a lot of straight guys and nervous first timers will use the escort route as it is by far the easiest way to go rather than a hook up app or attending a bar or club. They may sound weird or whatever, nervous or hesitant when chatting to you by phone and you will have to discover a method of detecting who is genuine as opposed to the large number of dickheads that you will invariably attract.

If doing an incall you have the comfort & security of being in your own surroundings whereas an outcall you maybe more vulnerable but of course in that case it is easier to just leave or walk away if you feel unhappy and i have done that many times whereas at your place you have to ask him to leave which will normally be ok but may not. Just in case of the latter ensure all valuables, money etc. are put away and anything that could easily be broken like say laptops is also stowed away out of sight.

In the old days it was very common place to let a friend know where and who you are meeting purely for security and phoning immediately on arrival and departure from the session. For women and guys who are of little stature and cannot handle themselves as easily as others in a situation this can still be useful to employ (You also have the option of GPS location you or your friends can utilize). Nowadays you often see a picture of the client beforehand or can check him out on his socials, check the address online or even get him to send you his location in map form to your phone and all these things help you and hinder someone out to do you mischief or harm. You will also have his phone number for any follow up that is needed or indeed if you have to trace him or report to the Police. Many escorts do not take inquiries from withheld numbers but in my experience these are sometimes the best most discrete clients so i do take them but i am more on guard than normal as should you.

Timewasters have been discussed previously and that said the greatest majority of clients are great and genuine but of course there are horror stories like Boy George hand cuffing an escort to a radiator on to the well-publicized handful of serial killers that prey on young guys and sometimes escorts reported worldwide. If in any doubt, then just get up and go as there will always be other clients. You can help yourself in a stranger's house by taking your own water or drink with you and not drinking anything offered or accepting drugs off a client but i do not want to go over the top and scare you as this will limit your business and show up in your attitude. In decades of escorting i have had one mini fight, nothing of major stolen from my house and have left/cancelled many clients at both the phone call stage and during the meet itself. There is no pattern to the sessions i have walked out on as sometimes it is their attitude, sometimes it is obvious they do not have the money and at other times it is bad sex, bad breath, body odour etc. or just my gut telling me it is not meant to be...it has never been what the client looks like. Now, that said i am ex-military and an ex-cop so i imaging that if someone wants to dick an escort about or not pay him they may have not picked me to hire which is my good fortune. The fact is no client or amount of money is worth getting abused, upset over, mugged, raped or whatever for.

You can always have a can of mace or similar in your travel bag, weapons are not a good idea at all but you can get out of a bad situation if you have something lumpy to hand even a dildo. Bad clients do get reported to escort websites and online groups and it is wise to keep an eye on these as the perpetrators who maybe are unwell do tend to repeat the same pattern over and over again. Also, if you have a genuine issue not just 'the client had smelly feet or did not know how to douche properly' then be sure to report them online to help others. If you have real problems, contact the police if escorting is legal in your territory otherwise contact LBGTQ+ groups or indeed any other escorts you know who will help you. Basically, there is plenty of help out there for sex workers whatever the issue.

After timewasters the biggest issue is likely to be actually getting payment. Clients may wish to renegotiate when you arrive or equally have no intention of paying you at all. If you have doubts ask for the money on arrival (not my preferred method but i do it if i have payment concerns) or you can even ask for a deposit before the session (always before you travel any distance) or get them to send a UBER at their cost. Personally i never renegotiate as i find that rude & awkward and prefer to have a published known take it or leave it rate (This also helps when clients come back a year or so later saying last time you did it for say a hundred and fifty or so and you know that you only work at one figure so they are trying it on). What you are doing is playing the continual cat and mouse game of getting paid for your time and services and not taken advantage off. It does help that there are so many payment methods now from direct bank transfers to PayPal or you could get a mobile credit card machine. Be aware it is unlikely that you can get one of those payment machines for the adult industry so you may have to use some small subterfuge with the provider and of course for part time escorts the monthly fee may make them an unrealistic proposition. Besides all that cash is still king but these days you have to be set up for other methods as cash is slowly dying out for so many. Never accept cheques, future payments, promises, drugs in lieu of payment or excuses and if necessary go to the ATM or cashpoint with the client. If you feel you are never getting paid rather than enter a fight or major argument just leave and put it down to experience......it will happen occasionally but learn from it. If you are confident enough I have also been known to take a laptop or something similar and held it in exchange for the cash at a later date which often works....remember you are not the one at fault and deserve your agreed payment.

As mentioned earlier there are bad escorts, and clients also need to be aware of their security so much of the above applies to them. I have heard of big muscly escorts turning up at a client's doors and just demanding and getting the whole amount of money without stepping over the threshold. In fact, just mugging with menace. These guys are out there but the upside is that a client when he finds a good reliable escort, hopefully you, is much more likely to stick and become a repeat client. There are sex worker Unions in some territories which you can pay to join but no one over-reaching body worldwide of note.....often most of their visibility is online. They can help you after the event with issues and have some good successes but also they can be talking shops, tied up in political sex worker rights campaigns or often leaning hugely over on the female sex trafficking side a long way away from most escorts actual experiences and concerns. Take a look online and see if you want to join or support these useful bodies if they operate in your territory staffed by good meaning people....there is a decent European one and one in the States but personally i am not an expert on this and have never joined one or even been asked to speak at one.

There are security implications and personal measures/decisions to take but it is a million times safer than it was just a couple of decades ago. Back then escorts had to linger on street corners throughout the night, climbing into strangers' cars or going into dark alleys and such putting themselves at considerable risk daily. Also, a lot of adult work which is now done from home is generally more accepted and queer bashing, violence against sex workers or stigma are hugely reduced. It is something to work on nowadays but hopefully if you are professional, have some good self-discipline & with some careful rules you will have very few actual security issues.

22 THE WIDER ADULT INDUSTRY

Escorting is a standalone business but can be readily enhanced and monetized utilizing many other aspects of the adult industry. This is just as relevant building your business and brand and leading up to a booking as following the session with add on's a long way away from the original meet.

The most obvious way and one we have referred to throughout this book is to become a celebrity in the fine art of adult movies. Simply porn stars are almost always the most highly sort after escorts. Of late due to a number of universal reasons like increased piracy, online saturation, every man and his dog having a camera at all times, free marketing on the web, fansites there is a huge amount of porn out there being produced daily. This means that generally the 'stars' and star power have diminished somewhat alongside the money that can be made from that sphere directly. Yet on the upside there are now so many more avenues you can pursue as an adult model or in effect an adult 'influencer' which can lead to financial gain. In some ways porn has become the ultimate and most powerful loss leader in that you don't make a fortune from it directly but you can use its massive exposure to really cash in big time as a whole. Basically, every model now is his own boss, business, company and brand and in my view 'exclusive contracts' with studios are as old fashioned and as much use nowadays as CD's and DVD's.

Therefore, apply to studios and web studios then do live appearances and when you have a following (which will come very fast) start your own JustForFans and Only fans subscription account. 'Fansites do not make stars, studios do' has become a well-known fact so you need to try and occasionally do some studio work to raise your profile beyond a couple of hundred guys spread globally that buy your individual content monthly as this small group is unlikely to boost your escort business greatly. A quick glance on social media like twitter will quickly underline how popular porn stars are and this can easily be monetized in the ways below but initially as an escort it makes you stand out from the competition, means you will be booked more often, recommended and be able to charge much higher rates per hour than none studio stars. There is nothing you cannot do with porn celebrity and once earned it can last a lifetime.

The general analogy that all models are now their own bosses, responsible for creating and maintaining their own brand and what to do with it now runs through a multitude of areas which can all become highly profitable. The aim should be to make money from clients you can physically meet but if that is not possible due to location, distance and time you now have other ways to make things work financially.

One question is what makes a star or someone that can make money from merely who they are. The International recognized figure of what makes an 'influencer' is if you have over 10,000 followers online. For anyone who does studio or web studio scenes occasionally this target can be reached in just a couple of weeks. Therefore, if that is you what else can you do with your new 'influence'.

Camming - Over the last 20 years adult performers with a presence can charge for pre-advertised live group online meets which is a big industry in itself and like many of the areas in this chapter particularly come into their own with customers who do not live in liberal or urban areas where the web becomes their main outlet and a real meet is largely a pipe dream. This is a great way to make money from a number of clients wherever located at once.

Adult Video Messaging & Cameos - A very new and successful area where you provide pre-recorded messages to individuals wishing them a happy birthday or discussing something more personal maybe. You can often get a couple of hundred dollars for 30 seconds of work......if you can create demand.

Fansites - Only Fans, JustForFans and the many other similar sites have arrived in the last 7 years. You just need to film parts of your life and charge a monthly fee for people to access it and feel close to you. It is often described basically as 'paid twitter'. The more sexual you make it the more lucrative it will be unless you are in other areas like personal training, cooking or a mainstream celebrity like Justin Bieber or Cardi B. There is an interesting modern situation occurring nowadays where fit guys can choose who they have sex with (Somebody they consider hot/horny), film it and post on both their personal fansites for cash. It is too early to tell how this will pan out as the whole world and his wife now seems to have an Only Fans account many of which include very average, poorly lit, badly edited, uncast rushed clips with poor audio but could this in some way start replacing some escort availability as why have sex with someone you do not fancy for money when you can nowadays have sex with someone you do fancy.....watch this space on how this develops and whether the fansite bubble bursts or indeed the escort one does or they are mutually helpful to each other as is the case now.

Streaming platforms - These are places like RawFuckClub where you can post any filmed sex you have and get a one off or repeat fee and can include areas of the 'free hub platforms' like Pornhub also.

Own website - Make your own site to market all that you offer and drive clients of all shades towards anything you have for sale. Two of the best companies to help you in this regard are Studio Presse and OLB (Online Buddies).

Sugar daddies - Older guys who like to spoil younger, celebrity or fit escorts with gifts, holidays and possibly cars and houses. These can sometimes last many many years.

Cash Masters or Findom - This is where you charge customers to feel subservient and pay money or 'Tributes' to be effectively physically and verbally abused online.

Hosting & live appearances - These are great fun and have gone on since the birth of the adult industry - you will need a personality and confidence though and the basic theory of whether this will work or not is does your name or image attached to an event or appearance sell tickets on the door?....which equally applies to the next category.

Live sex shows - pretty obvious in that you are paid to perform sex acts at a club or bar. This is fantastic for publicity for your brand as venues will post many adverts and posters all carrying your image and name without costing you anything. Alternatively there is being a gogo dancer which often relies more on gaining tips from clients at a venue.

Selling branded clothing - Experts always say to not be too clever and always start with baseball caps and Tee-shirts before, if successful moving onto other more exotic items.

Sponsorship - You may get sponsorship from companies or individuals the latter is particularly prevalent in the muscle worship world.

Company support - Retailers love their products and clothes being used, worn and posted about online. They will send you so much stuff if you are a successful adult performer and all you have to do is post a nice clip on your socials or get some selfies out and about in their gear. The pure 100% definition of an 'influencer'.

Your own dildo, sex toy or general merchandise - Big stars will be approached by major players like say Doc Johnson otherwise you can get your own dildo done or forge a relationship with a retailer you favour. Like the next 4 suggestions the mark-up is absolutely massive. The cost of producing being very little whilst the price as an 'adult celebrity' you can sell at maybe 40 or 80 times greater. In effect the profits are fucking huge and you have the dream scenario where you are in effect 'making money whilst you sleep'. Maybe sign any goods sent or send a picture with you holding it or wearing it.

Selling used underwear - Pants, speedos, kickers and especially jock straps are huge sellers. Wear them for a few days especially somewhere sweaty like the gym as it is the smell and look that customers are paying for. Buy a pack of 3 and sell them a week later with a massive mark-up as described above. For authenticity maybe send a picture of you wearing them.

Selling bottles of your semen - Little files of your baby batter can be collected and sold the world over for possibly 100 bucks plus. Maybe take a picture of you holding it and send a personal message to your fan collector and wait for the repeat business.

Selling bottles of your piss - Sames as above but even easier to produce, transport and often even more popular. I have never in my life found an easier way to make big money than this.

Write a book or produce a calendar - Armies of adult stars have gone before down this route and the reason is it works and makes money. Calendars are easy but book writing needs skills so maybe consider a ghost writer.

Controversies - These always can be turned into money making opportunities or incredible publicity stunts - be creative but beware there are often backlashes so you may need a thick skin especially if you end up bringing the LGBTQ+ or sex worker communities into disrepute.

Interviews - adult celebrities are always in demand for interviews. Many are unpaid yet great for publicity but paying gigs are out there.

TV appearances - Mainstream media is fascinated by the adult industry simply because their viewers are dirty bastards and just cannot get enough of it. Therefore, you will hopefully be asked a few times to appear in some sort of documentary which more often than not will be paid but regardless the publicity and claim to fame afterwards is invaluable from being on something like the BBC or Netflix. Be aware that you have no control as to who will see it and this may include elderly relations, your children in later life, past teachers, ex's or religious friends etc. so any right to privacy or keeping personal discretion can easily go out the window. I recently bumped into a Netflix crew following around the well-known adult model Bastian Karim and this type of exposure on release will be invaluable for him.

.......and basically, whatever you can dream up that suits your specific angle or niche of the business. Purely and simply the perfect escort/adult industry worker will nowadays do all of the above and become their own little cottage industry maybe even getting a helper or part-time assistant to ease the burden. The end result can be stunningly lucrative and could last for many many years and even decades if handled correctly. Some adult studios have stopped selling films and now make all their money from merchandise alone that side is so lucrative. You can put all your business areas on one Link Tree page online or/and get your own one stop website.

23 FETISH & SERVICES

You can offer any service you are comfortable with and that you think you can sell plus are prepared to do and do well. This in effect means that everything is up for consideration. The more you offer the more clients and cash you will get and niche areas can command a premium or just by definition have much less competition and are easier to get noticed with. Fetish areas or cleverly thought-out services especially those that go with your look have been mainstays in the industry since forever. Even if not into them and not advertising them you will still be asked sometimes if you would consider it so you need to take a view or stance on your limits clearly in your head.

Limits will exist for both parties you can make it clear what you do not offer or are into with your marketing or during the booking but it is unlikely that you will discuss everything so likely to come up in the session too. Do not be talked into something you are uncomfortable with ever. This is one reason why abstention from drink or chems on the job will stand you in very good stead. If you don't do bareback, kiss or like being restrained then do not do it. I am a total top and have been asked to bottom many times and sometimes for a lot of money but I have always stood my ground for both escorting as well as filmed or live appearances. Your client will also have his limits and he may be quite inexperienced so discuss it with him and try to read him. Often, they have huge fantasies in their head which in real life they just cannot handle. In my experience this is most common in something like corporal punishment when they ask for 500 strokes with a cane as hard as possible and no safety words and are bailing out at stroke number 6 for example. The opposite can happen too and it is fun to offer things to a client he has not experienced safely and consensually and maybe he really gets into it.....he will certainly remember you. The number of clients that say they are not into rimming and after a fun bit of play within the hour they are licking you out deep like an empty yoghurt carton. Likewise, the experience a client gets which i have witnessed many times when they get fucked for the very first time, or take a fist or double penetrated will stay with him forever and he will be back hiring you again in no time......sometimes the following day. Personally, i avoid taking bookings from the same client in one week as it means they are getting obsessed with you which will be problematic and will speed up their eventual decision to move on (The exception to this is if they are just visiting your location for a short time). Also of course it is a useful way for you yourself to stop getting bored of the job and feeling as though you are a number or on a production line.

If doing anything in the fetish area you should agree a safety word at the start which if the client utters stops the session immediately and allows you both to regroup. No safety words may be horny and exciting to some clients but it is risky as a lot of the heart of the session is around communication between both parties. As a top the client wants me to be in control and maybe be verbal, aggressive and dominant which is easy for me having all the power but as the client is paying you need him to have the session he wants and to what level which means he has just as much power. You need to try and ease your way through this which may require a bit of acting.

Fetishes and Niches come in two areas. Of course, firstly a fetish can be a type of gear, role play or mind games. Clients maybe into the fetish of leather, daddy/son, uniform, workman, sports captain, suited boss, school teacher, prison guard or whatever and there are as many areas of this type of fetish as people's minds can dream up. Secondly, there is fetish sex acts which tend to be defined as anything beyond vanilla sex. So, some may consider barebacking a fetish, while others are into BDSM, toe sucking, drinking piss, fisting, bondage, asphyxiation play, milking, fuck machines etc. so just need to get your head around both these 'fetish' definitions early on. I tend to class number 1 above as a fetish and number 2 above as a niche service. It just needs discussing in the booking or early session stage. Even better if you can get it into your marketing profile, description or image portfolio your business should boom. Niche's and Fetish's are big business and not offered by the great majority of escorts so this is a fantastic area to explore and develop your business accordingly over time.

Even if you are not particularly into fisting, cp or piss offer it if you can see it through. The onus is usually on the escort to have the equipment so you may need to invest in say gloves, canes, water expulsion pills, restraints, slings or whatever to provide the scene the client has booked you for. If there is anything you won't do like say 'brown' in my case i.e. shit, make this clear over the phone beforehand. Many clients will appreciate some gear maybe leather, rubber, sports kit whatever, so offer these scenes which will help bookings or offer them when you get repeat bookings to add some flavour. Also consider father/son scenes, teacher/pupil, officer/recruit role play basically whatever fits your look, build, attitude, age, body type. Be creative and find a market that works for you as I guarantee there are clients out there for absolutely everything......one of the worst I had (besides the illegal requests you will get for underage and bestiality) which i turned down was to masturbate myself on the side if a canal whilst the client drowned himself.....go figure!!.

24 ESCORT TALES - JAFAR XXX

I escorted for a bit when I first started doing porn. Had very mixed experiences. First being the worst. The client was very demanding whilst being on a low budget. He wanted the whole shebang in half an hour & usually I take that much time with foreplay. I work at my pace and being mentally so dominant I like doing what I want to do not what someone's asking for, no matter the circumstances.

That kind of put me off at first but then I did meet some very chilled clients where I would sit down have a drink & a chat which makes it a lot easier for me to connect with someone. Often i am at a clients having a very deep & interesting conversation which was great. All in all it was good money and I was happy when doing it and it was very enjoyable and easily paid my bills but nowadays i am so busy working hard to make quality content for my fan sites and do more studio shoots that i struggle to fit it into my schedule. The good thing is that it is always there as a backup job whether part-time or otherwise anytime i need it and once you have an established name it is so easy to pop in and out of that line of work whenever suits as almost every day i get inquiries i cannot action even without marketing in that area specifically.

25 CELEBRITIES & DISCRETION

There are pretty obvious and clear reasons why celebrities and for that matter wealthy guys who own business's or have some other sort of high profile use the escort route. They are horny like the rest of us and even better they have the money and often limited spare time so an escort is the perfect answer. Also, it is virtually impossible for them to visit nightclubs, saunas, sex clubs or cruising areas like the rest of us and just as hard to use hook up apps or websites. Therefore, in my experience of the great and good from the movie, entertainment, sports, politics, titled or corporate world these guys tend to be very regular hirers and generally pretty inexperienced sexually with not being able to go through the repeat Friday and Saturday night rituals and rights of passages that the rest of us were & are able too. The lack of access celebrities have had too any form of casual sex or company used to be problematic due to the newspapers but nowadays is greatly increased by the proliferation of mobile phone and cameras meaning they have to be hyper careful everywhere. You try taking George Michael to a sex club and see what hoops you have to jump through to protect him from unwanted publicity especially online when all he wants to do is have fun like anyone else.

You cannot target this market but instead they will find you and will regularly and understandably use false names and looks. It is always best not to make a fuss out of them and treat them like any other client which they will largely appreciate.

What this group wants is discretion which often applies to many clients not in the limelight who just have partners, relationships or are in certain jobs. Therefore, making a big deal and getting a reputation for discretion will do you the world of good in a great, fun repeat market where money is usually the last consideration. You could charge extra but personally I have never done so out of respect to them which may be a factor in my own success in this market. As mentioned previously this world is renowned for passing contact numbers around between them which helps your marketing bill and means that these 'new' clients want you and only you not so much for your look or cock size say but wholly for your reliability and ability to be discrete.

Sometimes they will get close friends to 'review' an escort beforehand but otherwise it will be done directly. One factor that has helped recently is that the 'outing' of men who hire escorts or who are gay is now not really seen as news by the media or indeed general public but they still tend to be careful and discrete. Back in the early noughties i first became aware of the 'Big Seven' which were very well-known male

Hollywood film stars that regularly hired escorts when on tour filming or press promotion away from Southern California. These were well known in elite escort circles and over time the group has changed with new names added and others relegated somewhat. My first experience of one of these was when i got a call from a guy asking my availability many weeks ahead which was slightly strange. It turned out that this was the actors PA who regularly booked escorts ahead for his boss. The story used was that he was about to do a cop acting roll and wanted to meet me which seemed very tenuous and unlikely. Three phone calls later with other members of staff including weirdly a woman and a very heavy legal one with non-disclosure documents to sign before it was all confirmed. I had to keep the whole of that particular weekend he was in London on stand-by with a nice financial retainer for my trouble in case the client found a window for play in his schedule. Eventually we had a very bland 2-hour session for which i was paid almost quadruple my weekend rate. This example of the 'top end' of the business indicates how lucrative this market is and how important it is to build a professional and discrete brand long term. Two years later his manager also hired me for a night so it sure works to be business-like and then another member of his staff so maintain your reputation and therefore your clients over time it will pay dividends. As mentioned before sports men (Especially soccer players and rugby pro's) certainly pass around escorts details surreptitiously in their teams or wider to colleagues and actors seem to have the same clandestine system. Once you fuck one you will get more for sure often quite quickly.

They are to be honest normal inexperienced cashed up guys who invariably are some of the easiest and best clients and they are great fun notches to have on your bedpost. In my experience they tend to be heavier into fantasies and such which if catered for by you will mean you are more likely to crack this market repeatedly. It seems their lack of sexual opportunities and the aforementioned experience means that they tend to build up fantasy scenarios presumably dreamt up through a million sessions of frustrated wanking & self abuse. So, expect cop scenarios, suited interview scenarios, mock rape and domination, military, prison, sportswear (Really Especially Sports team fanatasies!!), leather etc scenes from those in this sphere and soon you will probably have a string of film stars, musicians, TV personalities and elite sportsmen with you on speed dial.

26 REPEAT CLIENTS AND LONGEVITY

This section should possibly be a summary of everything we have said before. If you provide a great service, are professional, on time etc. and you both have fun and enjoy each other's company then they will whenever in your locale rebook you. Repeat clients fill up your dance cards faster than anything else over time and often want longer sessions and before you know it you have a very lucrative successful career for as long as you want. Provided you adapt and keep your business current with fresh pictures, descriptions and services then you will have achieved the golden goose of longevity. Ultimately you can reach the position where you no longer have to advertise as you have a string of regulars.

If you enjoy sex are confident, fun and outgoing and like meeting new people you have found the right job for you, basically. The aim is to get happy repeat clients which means always turn up, be professional, never do chems (you are 'working' after all) and even if you don't fancy the guy give him the best time you can, remember you are being paid handsomely for just 60 minutes just imagine it is Chris Hemsworth's, Lautner or Ronaldo (personally my go to fantasy if needed on the job is topping Jason Statham).

Establish a relationship with other escorts who will pass on their overflow work and get you involved in duo, group or escort tag-team or fantasy sessions. Word of mouth is extremely helpful & many guys will tell their friends that you are a great shag and next time they should book you. Build your brand up in any way you can. The most common of which is start working in porn. If guys have seen you on film then they will want you and only you and often search for guys by name booking weeks and months in advance or traveling specially because they want to taste or feel your cock or flying you to them. If you have a porn persona you may not be the most hung guy in your city or with the best body but you will undoubtedly be the most booked guy and you can charge what you like or at very least way above the average rate. Not all porn stars do escort of course many guys such as Brent Everett, Francois Sagat, Hans Berlin or Rocco Steele choose not to for various reasons often because they just don't fancy it, make enough money other ways or they have partners who don't like the idea but they are all aware of the huge amount of money they are foregoing and it is always available to them if they choose to one day.

Longevity and a career should be within your grasp but your life will change. Your attitude to anonymous sex may diminish or the mentality that you only fuck for cash might stifle your prospects of finding a partner. Your relationship status will invariably change and although some partners may get off on having a in demand boyfriend others may have big issues with it. So, it is a constant ever-changing picture that will need ongoing work. At the very least once you have done it for the first time successfully you can leave and return to the industry anytime as time, events, financial issues or relationships change.

Age is the one big factor you will have to keep abreast off. There are escorts in their teens (legally) and others doing well in retirement age. Yet the services they offer will be very different. You can get away with just being cute at 20 but 10 years later you will lose business to new cuter guys on the block. Therefore, you will need to change your service as time goes on. Maybe making and advertising yourself in a more masculine way, say with facial hair or more fetish. Maybe make a feature of your hairy ass, embrace the terms bear, daddy or mature as rather than being negatives to those who just want youngsters, they will become huge positives to a whole new range of clients. Constantly review your service, marketing, images and target audience. Add other things that you may get into overtime like BDSM, Corporal punishment, electro, watersports, roleplay, fisting, foot or muscle worship etc and keep your never-ending gravy train of money coming in. Of course, there is other extensions you can move into like an Only fans page, porn movies, clothe modelling, cam and live work and the wide area of merchandise or cash master/subs.

This is the first generation where we can have lifetime escorts who truly have a long happy career if they move with the times and mutate their services accordingly and with the ever-improving improvements towards legality there has never been a better, happier more lucrative time to be in the oldest industry in the World.

27 TIPPING

Escorting is the sort of service which is heavily skewed towards tipping. It is an expensive service so do not expect it every time and of course do not ask for it. That said there is so many bad escorts out there (I tend to think 3 out of 5 on average) that a client will appreciate a great service and there are so many opportunities to go above and beyond. Also within reason do not clock watch and a extra 15 or 20 minutes never hurts as opposed to kicking him out during the 59th minute of the session. Other things include offering him a drink, getting him relaxed, being engaging and entertaining to suggesting areas that may interest him not previously discussed or maybe that he has never tried. If you are doing a good job you should often be getting 20-50 bucks extra as a tip. Nowadays with PayPal and bank transfers etc cash is becoming less common which as a tip will come at the end of the session may meaning this could happen less and less.

Clients especially repeat ones will often want to bring you gifts, which maybe bottles of wine, small presents, clothing they may want to see you in, sex toys to use and keep or maybe something random you were talking about in your previous session. One client of mine regularly brings me very fancy designer cheese that he knows I like another bought me a full range of clothing from a fetish retailer called 'Slick-it-up' which must have cost him a few thousand. If you are good at the job clients may become obsessed with you. This in a bad stalkerish way is to be avoided but more readily they will just want to please you and feel like you are friends. This can lead to a great evening out, weekends away (paid), overseas trips whether business for them or holidays (again paid) and large expensive gifts like watches, jewellery, tech or whatever. Some are given cars by their clients and others have been given flats and houses even. More straightforwardly you should open a 'Wishlist' on Amazon with 40 or 50 things you would like say nice shoes, a designer hat, neck chain, mobile phone, picture etc that you can leave out there for clients to dip in and out of as and when. There is nothing nicer than receiving a free unsolicited gift in the post from a regular client. Just take a picture of it and send him a horny thank you message and hopefully more nice goodies will come in time.

28 HEALTH

Regardless of whether you are an escort or not your sexual and general health should be all important to you. Let's split this up into 4 mini sections.

1   HIV - Since HIV and AIDS has come on the scene in 1980 this has been a major issue for gay men and escorts. Originally wrongly labelled by some as the gay plague it was back then somewhat associated with the gay world but thank goodness now in more enlightened times that stigma has moved away largely. HIV which if not treated can lead to AIDS and severe illness or death. It is caught through the exchange of bodily fluids when the infection comes into contact with your blood stream. Very basically, it can be transmitted through penetrative sex either in a pussy or ass or via oral sex which is harder to transmit but does happen.

    For over a decade now we have had treatments like PrEP, PEP etc. which can in almost all cases stop transmission and even better keep those with HIV very fit, well and living long, fully extended lives. As of today, there is still no formal cure for AIDS just very successful infection management. Therefore, for the last 40 years condoms have been a necessity for gay and straight escorts and sometimes even the use of things like dental dams for blow jobs. Yet, for many both giver and taker they form a barrier, feel fiddly, artificial etc. and so nowadays very commonly they have fallen out of use somewhat in favour of unprotected sex as medication has taken over somewhat. PrEP etc is so readily available for those that are sexually active and into repeat anonymous sex that bareback is now by a long way the most requested and supplied in the escort world rightly or wrongly. So, the majority of escorts for their own health tend to be on PrEP or should at least seriously consider it. This means that they cannot contract HIV or indeed the similar big nasty HepC (Which is also now at last also treatable). As all your clients will be adults it is likely that many of them will also be on PrEP so in effect HIV as a topic has been somewhat removed from the escort debate. In addition, escorts or indeed clients who are Poz (Positive with HIV/Have HIV) will be on medication and are almost certainly undetectable. The slogan U=U means undetectable = Un-transmittable which means that you cannot catch HIV from them and in fact they are probably the safest fucks as you will not catch anything serious from Poz guys and they are arguably safer than Negative guys because at least they know their current and up-to-date status. So, you can escort or hire a HIV guy with great piece of mind these days provided you have taken the sensible adult precautions available to those into anonymous sex. In many ways PrEP has replaced the role of the condom meaning more natural feeling sex with less hassle and a sometimes awkward unsexy moment or discussion that used to occur in the midst or beginning of the session. Of course, women have other considerations and contraceptive methods to deal with to avoid possible pregnancy.

2   OTHER SEXUAL TRANSMITTED DISEASES - These often referred to as STD's or STI's include some well-known problems like Gonorrhea, syphilis, chlamydia and others. They have always been around; you will catch them occasionally and are all very easily treated. Obviously, you do not want to transmit any of these to your clients so after a quick visit to your local clinic or doctor a couple of tablets you will merely be abstaining from all sex including with your partner for a few days. These are not terminal, more an inconvenience and an unavoidable issue which comes with the job ofr being sexually active. The end result is that you will have to shut down your business as an escort for a week or so which means a financial loss and maybe some cancellations. Just build it into your mind set that this will happen randomly, is no great headache and enables you to have a few days away from the job and also ensure you put some money aside from your much, much longer healthy times to see you through these short hiccup periods.

3   DRUGS AND CHEMS - These are illegal and could have dangers for you in that regard especially if you are supplying them to clients however casually as you will be classed as a drug dealer. They also tend to mean your guard is down and you may not be thinking straight which means that you may do some sex acts you are not into, you may be abused in some way, you will not be in working and professional

mode as you will be 'partying' and make mistakes as regards getting paid etc. Without question your time control will go out of the window and you will spend a lot longer with a client probably many hours that you won't be paid for.....your time is money and valuable and chems work directly against this. Easiest thing is to avoid all chems in effectively your workplace and also offered to you during a booking is dangerous for your security let alone your health and invariably your performance will suffer on that job and probably those on the subsequent days too.

Many clients will supply chems which you can turn down or take. Basically, i have been offered everything often several times a week and if i took them my business and personal life would be in the toilet, my health would be destroyed and most likely i would probably be dead. It is tough as drugs and sex are close bedfellows for many maybe a bit more straight forward for someone partying or getting 'high and horny' (HnH) once a month for sex but for an escort this could and may come up daily and has the potential to really fuck you and everything up big time. Many clients only contact you as they want drugs supplied rather than sex or company and if you don't you will lose that client...no loss. Likewise, they may want to be 'on the same plain' as the escort so will want you to 'party' with them which is not really the deal but that is your choice but i would argue that is the start of the slippery slope to long-term failure in the industry. I can assure you good readers that all the top escorts and those with careers and longevity are pretty strict on themselves not doing drugs in effect their workplace. I am not here to preach and you will have to work your own way around this issue with your own rules which will unquestionably & repeatedly arise almost every week. If it helps i usually in interviews put my success and longevity firstly down to never doing chems and that has worked for me well and hopefully this stance will do you good also. I have lost clients who want a supplier and equally those that want someone to get high with but there is always another client around the corner and with that one i won't lose a couple of days work or socializing coming through a long drawn out unhealthy come down. I have had thousands of clients that have done drugs during our session including off my cock, ball sack and ass but have always by abstaining myself kept control and have left the session on time, with full payment and no hangovers and industry induced spiraling habits. Also, speaking as a top, chems do make some guys horny but invariably they are unable to get hard themselves and cum which of course is often what they want from me so is the best reason for abstention. As a pro they also tend to make the conversation and company by the minute less intelligent and i firmly subscribe to the cliche that 'chems never ever made anyone more interesting!'. I have also known countless young fit escorts who have lost their lives well before their time and 90% of the cases drugs are a factor if not the dominant one. Which brings us to number 4.

4   DRINK & ALCOHOL - Really, so much of number 3 above can be repeated here. Drink is in effect a legal drug and i love it away from the job. Yet, it is not for the workplace, will mean your guard is

lowered together with your professionalism and invariably long-term has just as many health, addiction and social problems as chems for you if over indulged. We all know from the age of 18 that drinking kills our boners which off course means you cannot cum, wank, fuck or whatever. In effect drinking turns you into a bad unprofessional escort who cannot perform, satisfy and actually do his job. I once had a great repeat client who wanted a second top so he invited over this other escort who could not get hard at all & did not cum. After 30 minutes the client asked him to leave with a much-reduced fee and of course never booked him again. I went downstairs with the escort and he said that he had just had half a bottle of Vodka to which i replied then maybe you should not have taken the job as a top?. He then said he thought i would have Viagra i could give him as he did not have himself the old stand-by and expected me to prop up his bad business performance. I checked a month later and he had left the industry.....so much for longevity and professionalism!. Whether you like drink or drugs in private they should be kept far away from your job and workplace and due to its proximity to escorting & the social situation around this profession it then is even more important to have clear boundaries and personal rules in this job. Of course, if you are dining with a client beforehand he may want you to drink with him which is fine just make it clear that this will have a knock-on effect with performance afterwards possibly.

Also guard against someone paying for an hour and then trying to 'trick' you into spending the whole of the night for free by getting you high or inebriated. There is also a medical issue with taking Viagra or similar alongside chems or alcohol which medical professionals would strongly argue against. Always taking Viagra with clients will lead to a dependency on it for every sexual encounter which is not good. Also, if you inject your cock with the likes of Trimix or Caverject for an extended erection then be aware of the health risks their especially if your cock will not go down a few hours later. It may sound great but it is in effect painful and dangerous for your health and may require a trip to your local accident & emergency hospital. Personally, i have injected my cock (which is a very small pin and less painful than it sounds) only for live sex shows on stage or filming not for escorting - firstly it is pricey at say $30 a shot per client and secondly as your cock is desensitized it is much much harder to actually cum with.

29 ESCORT TALES -
MARC McAULAY

My first escort experience and the one that got me
hooked into the business was a pretty straight forward
innocent affair. It was with a famous guy from the horse
racing world that i had seen on the BBC many times and
to be honest i found him to be a bit of a creep and did
not fancy him at all. It could have put me off escorting
as a whole with hindsight. I did not know it was an
out and out escort situation as i fancied the young lad
he was with and the older guy said it was his work
colleague which seemed a very unlikely story as he just
did not look the part and knew nothing about horses
and racing. He took us both to a fancy hotel and me
and the lad got it on and it was hot. The old guy who
was loving watching it came over and said keep going
Marc i will look after you and started giving me £50
notes. He then began rimming me before watching me
and the lad play some more. The next morning he said
that i was his favourite guy as he loved the porn i had
done for the gay sexual & torment studio called Straight
Hell which he had obviously seen......which is weird as
due to legislation it is not possible to view that porn in
the UK. He then paid me more than the young lad and
then i worked out the whole scenario was effectively

2 paid escorts for the night and he was largely a voyeur who liked jerking off watching guys having live sex. He also paid my Cab home and gave me a tip. So, without prior advertising or any intention of becoming an escort as i was a serving member of the British military i fell into it by default. Loved it and especially the ease and amount of cash available so started organising it more formally.

30 THE PRO'S & CON'S OF ESCORTING

WHAT ARE THE BEST THINGS ABOUT ESCORTING?

Loads of sex often with very fit guys and celebrities. The money is excellent and it will give you a lot of free time & other earning or quality of life possibilities. There is no qualification you need or special training and equipment and you can make it fit into your own time schedule. If you don't feel like working just don't answer the phone. You will get to travel and be entertained on someone else's dollar and you will be sort after by porn companies and club promoters with other work. Additionally, you will become a major attraction in any bar or club you visit off the clock, yes, your fun sex life will go up, way up !. It may also introduce you to your future boyfriend or many new mates who were originally clients. I infamously met and became the boyfriend of Alexander McQueen the fashion designer who was a former client. Harry Louis met his former celebrity boyfriend through the adult industry and there are numerous examples of guys starting full blown relationships with the great and the good remember many of the people who book you are multi-millionaires and need company like anyone else and if they have picked you from an advert amongst many then the attraction from one side at least is already a given.

With the rise of fansites like Only Fans, JustForFans, Many Vids, 4MyFans etc escorts nowadays have a travel or distance alternative to escorting. Sex workers now have the option of filming content with other models or sex workers of their choice and making regular money rather than the escort route being the only option. It means they can pick guys or girls they fancy to meet rather than possibly working with a client they are not attracted too as in the past. Add to this Camming and Adult Video Messaging then we have so many more options for sex workers than at any time prior. This could mean there is less competition for working escorts or indeed it might mean the standard of escorts available decline. Choice & ease of availability is a good thing though for suppliers and customers alike so a modern-day escort has more options of which direction to pursue and which to give a miss. One large bonus is that a sex worker can now make money from clients who are not in their vicinity for the first time and sex workers operating business like can achieve an awful lot more financially than before. Eventually many sex workers could make huge amounts per annum which will raise the profile of the industry greatly, make it look more attractive and legit and its detractors or critics look like they are living in the previous Century.

WHAT ARE THE WORST THINGS ABOUT ESCORTING ?

Every trading escort will answer this differently but one of the big gripes is timewasters. You will get so many calls, text's etc from guys just jerking off or having a cyber wank, maybe one in ten of guys who contact you turn into cash in your pocket so maybe avoid unlisted numbers. Some escorts end up with stalkers also and you are open to scammers 'I will send you a cheque in advance for your services you deduct the fee and send the remainder on to this Western Union account......' etc nonsense or cost you travel and time with no intention of ever meeting or paying. Remember - If it is too good to be true then it is, ALWAYS but you may end up on some film stars yacht just bide your time and stick to your own set of self-imposed rules religiously. You may also have family or relationship issues and boyfriend problems with the phone going in the middle of the night from someone who wants to have sex with you There is a well-known problem in the industry that escorts get addicted to cash for sex and that they then cannot get interested in sex without money changing hands and this should be avoided.....Escorting for cash can actually become an addiction. Once you go escorting it is also unadvisable to stand for politics or go into the Big Brother house or on TV for example as it will come back to haunt you. Security may also be a problem you are meeting strangers at their place often in the middle of the night or inviting them to your house so keep your wits about you and have systems in place. Do whatever checks you can and in your own place do whatever is necessary to stop people being light fingered or tempted. There are of course possible health downsides; some small like you will probably get an increased number of head colds or more seriously you stand a higher chance of catching STD's but of course nowadays due to medical advances everything you might catch is now curable or readily managed but at least these can put you out of business for an unexpected period.

There is a recent issue which seems to have arisen of late that due to facial recognition software used by authorities allegedly a couple of countries most notably the USA where escorting is not allowed reputedly do not allow Visas of entry to anyone that has ever escorted anytime in History anywhere whether perfectly legal in their home countries or not. This maybe an increasing problem for sex workers who are legally working & paying taxes in say Europe having problems visiting America for holidays as it seems the authorities blindly may presume you are there for work - sort of assumed guilty when innocent or pure guilt by association with the adult industry and surely a presumption of innocence should always be considered first and as a priority. In the future is the fact that you are LGBT say in Germany legally mean that you cannot travel say to somewhere like Uganda and Qatar as big brother CCTV is watching your every move and reporting your very existence to authorities who see you as undesirable. Obviously as the World gets smaller and travel more prevalent this maybe a short-lived problem, a non-issue, a blip or something which becomes a bigger thing in the future. If you have never broken the law in your own country why should another state presume you are a criminal before you even set foot on a plane. Laws change for sex workers in every country all the time and technology may create problems along these lines in the future but without doubt life is getting better for sex workers everywhere all the time and this is just something to keep an eye on and be aware of.

31 DO'S AND DON'TS - HOW TO HIRE A GAY FETISH ESCORT?

Just to balance things up here is a guide for clients which can also help escorts as to the mindset of what their customers want and have issues with.

Surely this is the most basic thing in a gay man's sex armory - IF YOU HAVE THE MONEY just simply call up a hugely fit guy with a massive cock and agree to meet, it couldn't be easier. Au Contraire there are so many things that can go wrong from you being robbed or arrested to you totally wasting your money or end up feeling shit and undesirable etc. On the other side escorts are the fittest, well hung and most fuckable men on planet earth and as they do sex for a living they will be hugely experienced maybe introduce you to some new things and you will undoubtedly have the greatest sex off your life with these guys, no question. Add into the mix that you may want a fetish service involving certain gear like cop, army etc or a special sex act like fisting to the bicep, being covered in piss, be tied up and beaten until your ass or back is marked or have a couple of bananas or dog chews pushed deep inside your hole. Then there are even more variations in the mix as to what can go right leading to the greatest orgasm of your life or wishing you had never got out of bed & on the phone that morning. Ultimately hiring an escort is most of all a convenience being what you want, when, with whom and without hassle.

Escorts always say they are selling their time and company which is what you are buying and what you two choose to do in that time is up to you as you may just want to chat, play Monopoly watch Ariana Grande videos or take a 14" cock and be pegged to within an inch of your life BUT..... YOU ARE NEVER PAYING FOR SEX....it just makes things easier for all. Of course, all good escorts know the business and know what is expected of them and invariably sex will be on the cards unless you are after a company, muscle worship etc type experience.

DO'S

1   Do spend a bit of time looking around the magazines or escort websites. There is plenty of choice in a City like say New York there are many 1000's of escorts available to hire at any time.....not all are on the opening page of a website so look deeper. If you want hairy, twink, oriental then keep looking until you find what really turns you on don't just phone up the first photoshopped manly chest you find. Be aware that the escorts who often pay money for top of list exposure are sometimes the worst to hire as to them it will be a numbers game, a production line with one out the back door as the next client comes through the front which is

hardly conducive to a memorable experience. Look further down the lists/pages for the quality guys that will treat you right, do not see you as just the 5th client of the day and make you feel special.... maybe even a boyfriend experience.

2   Ask loads and loads of questions as you are in control but do not come across as a cybersex timewaster. Do not just presume that every escort does everything. One of the most common mistakes is that clients don't ask if the escort kisses or not, equally if you want bareback or condoms then check. The type of sex acts are also useful to discuss especially in the fetish world if you want CBT, S&M, fisting, piss, beating then ask......shit for example (called brown) maybe not every escorts thing in fact undoubtedly not for the greatest majority. Many escorts won't even suck your dick or rim so best find out what you want before you end up in front of a gay for pay guy with endless dick collapsing instructions about no go areas. If you have any doubts, then politely move on to the next escort as in my experience if your gut has an issue or concern it is invariably right. Once you agree and do meet it is too late as you will be expected to pay some or probably all of what was agreed.

3   Some sites have review sections of variable quality so it's worth checking out. If a previous client has been treated with respect and taken time to post about it then you are on to a real quality cocksman. Remember that people are much quicker to write bad reviews than good so be aware if you come across a negative one or two as some clients can be total assholes and that escort could basically be a

good guy. Unfortunately escort reviews are far from ubiquitous and industry standard.

4   Be clean. Just because you are paying is no excuse for bad breath, B.O, or a dirty ass unless you are popping out of the office on your lunch break which is different and then you can ask the escort for a few minutes tidying up which he will always agree too. Of course, many fetish guys like body smells especially pits (see above in ask loads of questions). Do not ask the escort to not shower for that morning or clean his foreskin etc without paying extra for his time pandering to what you desire. Also try to be on time and if late its 2023 so text, WhatsApp or call as it stops the escort standing around in leather or boxing kit with a boner and will make the energy better when you do eventually meet. If you have to cancel or have no intention of meeting then let him know please.

5   Do ask for pics of things which interest you but be aware that escorts are plagued with dick pic collectors. If you are a top ask to see his ass, even open ass which let's face it is what you are paying for as it may be very hairy, spotty, smooth which works for you or not and then you can move on to another guy or book. Same for pics of cocks, feet, chest, biceps anything which is important to you. Of course, if an escort is not showing his face there is usually a reason and it's because he is more James Corden than James Bond or James Franco probably. In this day and age many escorts will have videos of them in action so feel free to ask and if they have done porn just ask for their name and google away and see if you are then ready to buy. Get the info

you need but don't pester the escort as they are busy guys and eventually one party or other will get wound up with endless questions.

6   Do agree the rate and don't try and re-negotiate. Escorts that are any good are between $150 and $300 per hour. Big name guys can charge what they like as there is only one of them but if they are over $500/hour then you might be into the world of expanded ego's and overhype. They are all available for more than one hour, overnights, weekends or overseas trips the latter two of course are open to some negotiation on hourly rates. Cash is king, cheques are a complete no no and of course nowadays we have Paypal, immediate bank transfers, and hand held credit card devices....but do check first. Maybe send half the rate in advance and do the rest when you get there. Some poorer escorts ask for the money on arrival but it is classier to get the money at the end and not even discuss it just put it down somewhere where he sees it. He wants repeat clients and you want a great escort to go back to that you can trust and grow sexually with, be relaxed and become acquaintances/friends possibly.

7   Do speak on the phone; texts, emails are not enough as you need to hear the guy's voice as he may sound pyscho or even worse as camp as a Drag Race winner. If in any doubts just don't go, just cancel if your dick is ruling your head and decision-making process or maybe leave the address with a mate or check in with a friend on arrival and departure or send your location. This security side is often overrated as incidents of being attacked or real problems are as rare as Putin telling the truth. Have

fun and take time. I know millions of escorts personally and they are great guys, superb company, fit as fuck, hugely intelligent, punctual, professional and brilliant at sex. They are not there for a relationship they are there purely for your adult entertainment/convenience and it is money very well spent where you will remember the sex for a long time unlike most Grindr/Scruff/Tinder time wasting rubbish hook-ups which probably won't happen anyway. Guys like Cutler X, Chad Brock and Dallas Steele have been doing it for a while and there is a reason for it they are great at their jobs and get many repeats. Poor escorts do not last in the business too long and the gay for pay ones who should be avoided at all costs have an even shorter lifespan.

DON'TS

1   Don't be a timewaster which has been the number one complaint by escorts for the last 50 years. If you want a meet go for it, most escorts will meet within an hour or two, later that day or the following day. If you are contacting them about a trip to their location next week or next Summer that is almost the same as saying i am a dick and i am jerking off whilst speaking to you over the phone and have no intention of ever booking you as i can hardly afford a Mars Bar. Every escort knows this as he will get 20 such calls a day. If you do need to book in advance because of travel then make this very clear and keep the questions at this stage to the minimum and business like and stay in touch continually without pestering.

2   Don't ask for duo's. This invariably means the escort will offer his boyfriend as the extra guy and you will be in the middle of one of those awkward three-ways where it is obvious two guys are more into each other than you and you are of course paying double to feel like the odd man out. If you want more than one guy at a time then book them as separate escorts and inform them of such - all good escorts will be happy with this as in honesty it is less work for them individually for the same money. Why should a escort take the trouble of booking a second or third guy for a client he does not know who may not turn up or be genuine....he will get his bf of bff and you will feel like a lemon. If you want a duo then you do the work for it for a more successful session.

3   If you live in a millionaire mansion then maybe do outcalls rather than incalls as an escort could increase the rate when he works out you are Elton John or Anderson Cooper but even more importantly it is the best way to avoid possible theft. We know of one celebrity who was charged 1500 bucks for a 40-minute shag as he did not discuss rates and the greedy escort had seen his gold discs on the wall......he was robbed of cash rather than goods as such. If you do outcalls to the escort if for any reason you are unhappy you can just leave offering part of the rate and never hear from him again or worry about him turning up at your place or stalking you. If you are just a normal bloke you may feel more comfortable having the escort in your own bed just don't leave any temptations out like mobiles, wallets, pictures of your boyfriend etc.

That said both incalls and outcalls are happening
every hour of every day equally successfully.

4 Don't let them film you with their big cock up your
ass when distracted unless this is your thing. This is
becoming more and more of a problem with guys
filming their own sex lives and charging for it on
monthly 'fans' sites such as the Only Fans and
JudtForFans for such content they should get your
permission and do some signed paper work & get
proof of age. These sites are perfect for the big gay
names with the likes of Austin Wolf, Armond Rizzo
and Rhyheim Shabazz pulling in mega bucks every
month which is great for these guys who have
effectively become self-employed successful porn
studios via 'paid for twitter'. The trouble is that
every guy now thinks he can do it and is filming
every single damn fuck, suck, shower they have and
posting it however average with any guy they can
find on Grindr/Scruff illegally. There are thousands
of cases of guys being filmed without their
knowledge or agreement and then suddenly it is
online for the world to see and someone else is
making money out of your ass getting fucked......
and then maybe your granny or boss finds it and all
hell breaks loose. Filming may of course not be
obvious to you. If you want to do porn then do it
just don't end up doing it by accident even pro porn
stars hired for these fan site clips are unpaid as it is
called 'content exchange' & is that worth having
your private parts all over the web badly lit, edited
and filmed without permission. Once filmed even
amateurly it is out there for life and may come back
to haunt you many years down the road.

5   Don't do chems. Chemsex is not big and not clever furthermore it is deadly in the escort world and stunningly unprofessional in what is in effect a place of work. There are so many reasons for this not least because escorting is more often than not legal/ignored by authorities whereas all chem activity is not. Chems ALWAYS result in floppy dicks and crappy sex too, so if you want someone to get high with do it with a mate or unpaid hook-up. Ultimately chems waste huge amounts of time where both the parties have no idea of the passage of the hours and with escorting you are effectively supposedly on the clock. So, if you want one poor screw in a 10-hour period for $2000 then go for it of course you will have to supply, take the risk and pay for the chems on top, alternatively the same escort one hour for one tenth of the cost and better sex, real natural connection and a hard dick..... this is not rocket science taking chems into effectively a guys work place which an escort is, is just plain dumbass.

6   Don't be judgmental about escorts and escorting. It is just a service of supply and demand. Basically, one guy has a 10" cock and the other wants it up his ass so it's like shopping for something you need or want. Escorts will also provide company, advise and do the sex acts that most hook-ups wont (and have the necessary equipment/toys). So, if you want to get fucked book a top and get fucked, if you want to lick a sportsman's feet then book him, get exactly what you want to avoid being two round holes with no square pegs in the room. Even worse don't look down on escorts they are not 'prostitutes'

'selling their bodies like whores' or any less than you or any other working Schmoe. This is not the 1970's or the dated straight mentality where paying for sex was 'only because you can't get it any other way'. Escorts are businessmen who are providing a service which we all need at some point when we have not pulled at a club or got horny in the office or when travelling for work & do not know your way around. It is an important business and if you avoid the bottom feeders is wholly full of very professional adult sex workers. Very fit, very successful and very good-looking men & women hire escorts as a convenience not out of desperation including many pro soccer and NFL players as do half of Hollywood, loads of politicians and the entire pop music world so you are in great company. The only two reasons why any man would not hire an escort is if he is in a monogamous relationship or simply does not have the spare cash.

7   Don't be the cops, Escorts are no longer plying their trade on the street being a 'public nuisance' & 'scaring children' as it is all done online or by phone in the privacy of adult's bedrooms so go and catch some real criminals or some dodgy American politicians or pedophile clergy and leave the hard-working escorts, sex workers and clients alone. There are no victims here and maybe get your laws out of the Victorian era into the 21st Century too. Also don't use withheld numbers as many escorts won't respond to them as they are the home of the timewaster and above all don't be a dick get the transaction done in a maximum of 3 texts and then lie back and enjoy Dolf Dietrich's or Silver Steeles

company. All your favourite stars are out there or your fantasy sex god or indeed guys offering things you just cannot find anywhere else, just one call away with their asses in the air awaiting for you so book your escorts wisely and sensibly, maybe share with your partner and watch your sex life hit a whole new fantastic level.

32 SO ARE YOU GONNA BE A GREAT ESCORT?

The job is made up of all types of guys and of all ages some but not all which are making some great money. For every 18year old hooking his way through college there is a 58-year-old doing great as a corporal punishment master. For every chubby bear escort there is a skinny skater punk selling his cock for 10 bucks per inch and all are having a good time doing it hopefully. Often escorting has the image of being depressing for desperate people, drugged up guys/losers who cannot get any other job but the truth is the exact opposite especially now with the WorldWideWeb, mobile phones. extra revenue sources and with much improved sexual health so most escorts have a great time and it is a wonderful confidence boost to know that guys want to sleep with you so much they are prepared to pay handsomely to do it (nothing depressing or to beat yourself up with there). In simple turns it is now a good career to have and follow. You can do it for a limited period just to get some cash for some specific reason like getting through college or renting your own flat or with continual adaptions to your business, marketing and ever-changing media it can last a lifetime easily and very successfully.

As a diversion here is a rough guide I wrote for a magazine in 2015 which hopefully you will find of interest of some top guys 'basic' advertised rates

HOW MUCH FOR AN HOUR OF 'COMPANY WITH YOUR FAVOURITE PORN STAR ESCORT

(These are 10 of the very top escorts on the planet available to you with just one phone call in roughly Euros and Dollars)

Austin Wolf - 400
Ryan Rose (Performer of the year 2015) - 350
Christian Wilde - 320
Rocco Steele 300
Boomer Banks - 280
Avi Dar - 250
Rafael Alencar - 250
Brian Bonds - 250
Cutler X - 250
Antonio Biaggi - 250

Many clients become good friends over time and you sleep very well at night knowing that as an escort providing entertainment, company and a partial 'psychologist' you have really helped some guys out or just made them happy for an hour or two.....and of course getting your bills paid along the way. Just consider Samuel Colt was flown across the world from America to China for just a weekend at someone else's cost whilst Ricky Sinz was paid once a year to sit on a boat in the Caribbean so what's not to like and what's to feel bad about IF you do the job properly and professionally. Escorting even had their own annual

Awards, the Hookies which stopped when Rentboy. com was Un ceremonially closed down. There are so many aspects, entry levels and dynamics to the industry that you can adapt to your own circumstances from just doing it say once a month to full time or from just offering company, phone sex or body worship through to a full on maybe slightly anonymous extreme sexual experience.

I have had the time of my life in the industry seen the world, had phenomenal experiences and met fantastic fascinating people including some huge celebrities (some of which you may be aware off & even dated a couple of them) had great fun and superb varied sexual encounters along the way. It has led through clients and other entities to many other business opportunities which have proved either lucrative or interesting and has enabled me to keep sane, happy, focused and not ever feel like I am on some sort of treadmill or that work is a repetitive uninteresting grind. I have made it a long-standing successful career, bought my house, paid off all debts, have a good standard of living, paid my taxes, had a million overseas trips and so can you.

There is such a massive gap from the here today gone tomorrow 6-week only trading escort who probably has done everything wrong as opposed to the long-lasting professionals whom will be following many of the rules and guidance laid out in this book and applying their own spin. Hopefully, this tome can help you be the latter and avoid many of the obvious pitfalls that can occur and therefore put people off the industry early on or drive them out of the business just after they cross the start line. You should think long and hard about what you can and want to offeror achieve and tailor your business to your own format. Not everything I have mentioned will work for everyone and you need to calculate when to do A, B & C or equally when to plan your own individual route that works better for you, your financial & living situation, your relationship, privacy & security, your goals and what areas you will mostly be successful in this incredible industry 'the oldest and most common one known to man'. Be proud of being a sex worker and bringing pleasure and happiness to people, hold your head high, have fun and never give yourself a hard time over your life choices or the odd bad booking. Look after your health, ask for advice from colleagues and your industry peers, work hard, keep your wits about you, invest some of your money, stay off drugs and drink especially when working and remember as a certain well-known drag queen says "If you don't love yourself, how in the hell you going to love somebody else - but darling never forget to collect that cash from the bedside table on your way out the door?".........or i am sure that is the advice that Mama Ru would give if asked on this matter.

Hopefully you can find me on social media, at public events/seminars/presentations or online if you have any questions, ideas or suggestions as I would love to hear from you and with that the happiest hooker that ever walked the earth now has to close the final page here and leave you with all my love, support and best safe wishes......and remember to tip, review and keep hold of my number! xxxx

PET SHOP BOYS - RENT - lyrics by Neil Tennant &
Chris Lowe.
"You phone me in the evening on hearsay
And bought me caviar
You took me to a restaurant off Broadway
To tell me who you are

We never-ever argue, we never calculate
The currency we've spent
(Ooooh) I love you, oh, you pay my rent."

www.ingramcontent.com/pod-product-compliance
Lightning Source LLC
LaVergne TN
LVHW011913080426
835508LV00007BA/504